TO JEANNIE & LLOYD

GOD [BLESS]!

William W. Norman

THERE IS STILL
POWER IN THE BLOOD

CONTENTS

This book is lovingly dedicated to my five beautiful granddaughters and my two rugged grandsons who will have to grow up in a world that is vastly different and much more evil than the world and times that I knew when I was growing up as a child!

May God's protection rest upon each of them, and may we all be united around God's throne in heaven one day!

FOREWORD

By Rev. Paul N. Papas II

I have been given the honor of writing a foreword to this very important and timeless book by Rev. Bill Woods.

Over the recent years, people have taken the events going on in this world and wondered if the world was about to end. We are living in the end-times; neither the author nor I can give you a date or time of Christ's second coming. If we knew that date, then we could tell you when the world would end.

This book may scare you, and you may wonder if the events in this book really happened. I was not there at the time, but the Holy Spirit verifies that this not fiction.

For those who belong to Christ, this book is a reminder that we should rejoice and give Him praises that we have been called out of darkness into His marvelous light, and we are protected by the God of heaven, our Creator.

For those who have yet to make a decision for Christ, this book is a great example of why you need to accept Christ as your savior.

The god of this world, Satan, is a defeated foe; and he wants to take as many people with him into the lake of fire as possible.

The good news is that each and every person gets to choose where to spend the rest of eternity, heaven or hell.

Take heed that Satan is prowling around to see whom he can devour.

We are assured that if we submit to God, our Creator, resist the devil, then the devil will flee. If you want proof of how that works, then you can believe the Bible, the basic instructions before leaving earth, which might seem like an old book to some; or you can believe Rev. Bill Woods in this book. He and his have wife lived through it. He wrote this to help others understand that spiritual warfare is real. He has helped many people who have been under attack by the devil and his followers. I am sure the devil is not happy with him.

Some think new age is new; not so, it is just repackaged from way back in time. You choose to worship the Creator or the creation. Anything that denies the sovereignty and supremacy of our Creator God serves and worships the creation. New age denies the supremacy of our Creator and worships the creation. The people Rev. Bill Woods was attacked by were not worshiping our Creator; they worshiped the devil and his followers.

Please pay attention to the events in this book, as you may, if you haven't already experienced the attacks of the devil or his followers. The good news is that there is victory with Jesus Christ!

Rev. Paul N. Papas II is the pastor and cofounder of a church called Narrow Path Ministries and the founder of the Family Renewal Center. Part of the mission of Narrow Path Ministries is to help bring hope to the lost; to help the abused, the abuser, and those affected by abuse to heal; and to be His hands and feet on earth until He comes.

The Family Renewal Center's mission is to break the cycle of abuse by healing the abused, the abuser, and those affected by abuse; providing stable, long-term housing and education for the abused and children in the West Valley of the Phoenix, Arizona, area, and rehabilitating the abuser.

INTRODUCTION

Why do we need another book *on spiritual warfare*? It seems the Christian bookstores are glutted with materials and books on this topic. What fantastic information do I have that will add to the knowledge that's already in print?

The fact is, God wants me to write this book because I am an ordinary pastor trying to lead my *"flock"* safely home to God's "fold." Like other pastors in today's church, I'm in the trenches facing problems and ordeals that seem unique to this generation. Today's pastors and churches are under open and blatant attack by demonic forces, which hasn't happened since Jesus walked on earth. In that generation, Satan tried to diffuse Christ's ministry because Jesus came to *set the captives free*. Satan didn't want Christ to succeed, so he did all he could to frustrate and discredit Christ's efforts by trying to compromise and destroy God's plan of salvation. He even went to the extent of having Jesus murdered on a cross. Satan thought he had somehow won, but this turned out to be a huge mistake because Jesus had to die as the atonement for our sins.

Ever since Jesus conquered sin, death, and the grave, Satan has tried to stop and defeat Christ's church. He has targeted pastors and strong Christian laypeople in an effort to destroy them and frustrate Christ's church. Satan will continue to fail. We must continue to battle him at every point and rescue souls from his clutches until we achieve our final victory and stand before the throne of God.

Today, Satan knows Jesus is coming back, and his time is running out. He's frantically trying to inflict all the damage he can to mankind while he still has time. The result is that Christians are dealing with more evil and destruction of the human soul than has been seen for many generations. The church must wake up, learn to combat, and overpower this demonic onslaught, or see millions of souls perish because we were too timid to take a stand for Jesus.

I am a pastor who served in the Church of the Nazarene for thirty-six years and am currently pastoring a Wesleyan church. I understand what it means to face opposition from Satan and his forces. I have been involved in deliverance ministry and warfare for several years. I offer this book as a *hands-on field guide* to Christians caught in the throws of spiritual warfare.

There is a lot of material on spiritual warfare in the bookstores, but very little of it offers *hands-on instruction* needed by those standing in the trenches. I hope this book will provide information, strength, direction, and encouragement to you as you minister for our Lord Jesus Christ. My prayer is that you will stand victoriously against whatever opposition Satan has to throw at you. The spiritual mortality rate of pastors in the twenty-first century is staggering.

In high school ROTC, they taught the students that there is no need for most of the casualties on the battlefield. Casualties come because someone has gotten careless and failed to take proper precautions. There is no need for casualties on the spiritual battlefield either when we fix our eyes on Jesus and determine to do His will.

Remember, we're not in this battle alone. Jesus is here with us. He has promised, "I am the vine, you are the branches. Without me you can do nothing" (John 15:5)!

Jesus has already sealed our victory with His blood on the cross, in the grave, and through the resurrection. Satan is a defeated foe. We are just involved in the "mop-up"—the real battle has been accomplished. We can be rest assured that *there is still power in the blood!*

Pastor, to answer my opening question: "Why do we need another book on spiritual warfare?" I have written this book to help you. You need to hear from someone who has been there and knows that Christ is faithful! *You can depend on Him!*

A DECLARATION OF WAR

Often people ask me, "How did you become involved in spiritual warfare?" My involvement happened long before I knew anything about deliverance ministries or demons or the pitfalls and consequences of taking an open stand against Satan.

I can relate to Jeremiah the prophet in so far as he was called before he was even born (Jer. 1:4-5). My maternal grandmother was praying that I would be a preacher or missionary from the time that I came from my mother's womb. When I was just a few months old, my dad was in the Philippines fighting for our country in World War II. He was under heavy enemy fire and assumed he was going to be killed. He bargained with God and promised God that if He would just get him out safely, he would give his infant son (me) to God to use in any way He saw fit. I've often thought how "big" that was of dear old Dad. He had his own life that he could've committed to Christ! He didn't become a Christian at this time, but he did come home alive. He always felt it was because of his bargain he made with God concerning me.

I grew up in the church. Every time the doors were opened, I was taken to church. I soon felt a love for the church and for God. My playtime as a small child was to stand and "preach" to my toys, the neighbor kids, my sister, or whoever would listen. By the time I was nine, I knew God had "called" me to a life of service for Him.

One incident stands out as being significant to my life. I was four years old. My family had been attending "revival meetings" at our church (First Church of the Nazarene in Walla Walla, Washington). The evangelist had preached a sermon about how Satan *dogs our track* all through this life and until we arrive at the pearly gates of heaven. He had mentioned that he believed that hell and Satan were contained in the midst of the earth and people who go hell are taken to a fiery mass located inside the earth. This made an impact on my four-year-old mind. I was still contemplating this information the next day as I was outside playing in my grandmother's yard. I was digging in one of her flower beds with a toy shovel when I hit something solid. I stuck my finger down to feel what I had hit. It was solid, kind of round, and had a sharp point! It was a rock, but to my childish mind, I was certain it was something much more sinister. I ran to the house shouting the whole way. I told Grandma that I'd been digging and had found the Devil's horn. It made perfect sense to me if the Devil lived under the earth. Grandma laughed and showed me that it was just a rock. It was then that I made the declaration of war against Satan that would change my whole life. I said, "Grandma, I hate the Devil! I want to live my life in such a way to hurt what he is doing in the world. When I die, I hope God will let me wear logging boots into the gates of heaven so that when I'm safe inside, I can turn around and give him swift kick in the teeth!"

Little did I know that Satan would take me seriously! I was serious, but who listens to four-year-olds? *Satan does!* I've been in a battle with him ever since that day when I was four. I still hate Satan and all that he does! I still petition God for the privilege to wear logging boots into heaven! I want to be in the lakeside leading the cheering when he gets thrown in the lake of fire!

I won't go into much detail about my earlier life here. I'll say that Satan has fought me at every turn. The first time I ever preached, I was sixteen years old. I preached at the Union Gospel Rescue Mission in Walla Walla, Washington. A man came forward at the invitation, and I was excited to have a seeker at my very first preaching assignment. When I went to pray with the man, he became very belligerent. He didn't want some "kid" praying with him. I tried to excuse myself when I saw his reaction and that made him madder. He ended up slapping my face. I don't have to tell you I was one very discouraged and disillusioned young servant of God. Satan had a heyday beating me up over that situation! He told me I could never make it as a preacher! The fact is I struggled over my call to preach because I just couldn't see how God could use anyone as backward as I was. Satan told me that God hadn't really called me to preach. I was doing it to please my grandma. Finally, on October 16, 1961, I locked myself in my dorm room at Northwest Nazarene College in Nampa, Idaho, and refused to come out until I'd settled this matter with God. God wonderfully confirmed His call upon my life, and I've never doubted my divine commission to this day!

Satan doesn't doubt it either!

My college career was quite bumpy at times. The enemy did everything he could think of to discourage me. I was in a car wreck that was the other driver's fault. He had no insurance, and my dad's car, which I'd borrowed, was totaled! The pressure from that episode just about ruined my junior year of college. Dad was riding me to replace his car; the owner of the other car was trying to sidestep his responsibilities, and the whole campus was taking sides on how the matter should be resolved (my side seemed the minority). My nerves and my grades went out the window! Finances were a constant conflict, but God was faithful and helped me through those times.

The best thing that God did to help me in my calling was to give me a wonderful and supportive wife! Without her, I probably wouldn't have made it this far. The problem is that she was brought in to this war with me.

Our ministry has always been difficult! Every church I've pastored has been in crisis. If I were to write the entire account, I'd be accused of writing dramatic fiction. But my purpose isn't to complain or have a "pity party." God is faithful! He strengthens and encourages us in any situation if we are there because of our walk with Him (Matt. 5:11-12).

I became most aware of my ongoing war with Satan and his forces when I was pastoring in Phoenix, Arizona. The church was buried in a building debt, which the congregation couldn't afford. I didn't know of the extent of this debt and the circumstances surrounding it until after I had assumed the responsibilities of pastor. The first board meeting I was asked, "Pastor, what are we going to do about the upcoming bond payment?"

"How much is it?" I asked.

"$28,000!" I was informed.

"How much do you have?" I asked.

"There's nothing put back, but you're the pastor, and we thought you'd have an answer as to how we can raise the money by the deadline."

No one had thought to inform me of this very stressful and critical situation when I had been interviewed for position as pastor of this church. I had asked during the interview if there was anything special that I should be aware of, and the people opted to keep this problem to themselves at that time. The information that I didn't have before my decision to become pastor was that the church owed $240,000 on their massive building program. It was a bond program. The payments were to be made twice a year: the fall payment was for the interest on the bonds; the spring payment was also for interest but included principal. The payments ranged from $7,500 to $28,000 and came due every six months! I had nearly thirty years of this pressure staring me in the face.

It was July 1980, when I was informed the next payment was due on September 15, 1980! I had less than three months to raise $28,000! I knew I was in trouble! Now I understood why this church couldn't hold a pastor for any length of time. The financial pressures were too great! I also guessed why they had failed to mention this small detail to me when I met with them at the interview.

People loved the program of the church. They liked the preaching, but they couldn't stand the constant pleas for money to meet the terrible obligations. No one ever stayed at that church and helped for any length of time.

It didn't help that there were other Nazarene churches with fine programs and less debt load within easy driving distance. Our church became a "holding tank" for people while they looked for another church where their pocketbooks could be less threatened. The standard greeting a visitor would give when welcomed to our church was, "Oh, we're just shopping. We're trying to find something to meet our needs." How strange, nobody seemed to need a heavy building debt!

As if that weren't enough load, I began having problems with some of the laymen who were disgruntled because God was convicting them through my preaching. It seems God often uses my pulpit to bring conviction, and then the people blame me and get mad at me. This has been a common problem for men of God throughout history. Anyone who has proclaimed the Word of God and taken a stand against sin has been unpopular with the world (John 15:18-24). It makes more sense to get mad at the messenger and the message than to openly be mad at God.

The church plant was quite large with five acres of buildings, yard, and parking lot. There were six separate buildings on the church campus. Finally, after I had been there for two years, it was decided to get a custodian to help keep the grounds and the buildings. He could live in a house on the property and receive a token wage in exchange for his work.

The first custodian we secured was lazy and undisciplined. He wasn't doing the work he'd agreed to do. When I confronted him that the work wasn't being done and I was receiving complaints about his job performance, he became angry and started a campaign against my leadership. He played like he was a martyr because he was expected to do the job he agreed to do.

He eventually took a job in Alaska and left his family in the house belonging to the church. He'd come back and get them in a couple of months when things were ready for them in Alaska. His wife and sons were supposed to maintain the janitorial work. They did no better at the upkeep than he had. Finally, I had to ask them to move so we could get someone that would care for the property.

The family complained to the congregation and the neighborhood about being put out of the house. You'd have thought I had moved them to the street. The fact was I'd given adequate time for the move. He finally came and took his family to their new home in Alaska. People were still disgruntled at me! Once a breach has been made (whether based on fact or a lie), it is very hard to put it right. Satan does all he can to fan the fire and keep the blaze going.

The new janitor wasn't any improvement! He cleaned the property better but decided to go beyond his bounds. One day, while cleaning my office, he noticed I had gas credit card statements lying on my desk. He went through them and found I was putting gas into both of my cars from that credit card. The credit card was provided by the church for my use to conduct church business. I had been given a $35.00 per-week limit to care for the business expenses that I would incur. I never reached the limit, but I did use both of my cars for the calling and running around doing business for the church. He spread gossip that I'd misused the credit card and was stealing from the church. *It wasn't true!* I wasn't even spending the amount I was entitled to spend.

He also found pop in a little refrigerator I kept in my office. The church had a pop machine in the fellowship hall, and my refrigerator had the same brand of pop in it as was in that pop machine! Of course, the only logical assumption was that I was stealing the pop! Further investigation revealed that I kept a nail keg in the office where I placed the empty pop cans! Nobody considered the fact that I knew where the grocery store was, and I might just be buying my own pop. He began to spread rumors that the pastor was stealing aluminum cans from the church!

One afternoon at 2:00 p.m., I received word that I was to call the church office. I called, and my secretary told me that I was to be in the office of the district superintendent at 5:00 p.m. that afternoon! This was going to put a kink in my schedule for the evening. I had a church board meeting slated for 7:00 p.m. The secretary said a group of laymen were bringing charges against me and meant to take my credentials. When I arrived at the district office, I was confronted by a dozen laypeople all in an irate mood. They wanted to see me lose my job, my church, and my credentials. The district superintendent saw through the ruse and dismissed the whole matter.

That evening at 7:00 p.m., about forty disgruntled, gossip-listening laypeople invaded our church board meeting and leveled all the charges at me again. The meeting lasted from 7:00 p.m. until 12:30 a.m. *It was awful!* Many people refused to believe that I had not done anything wrong and decided to leave the church because they couldn't sit under my leadership. Keep in mind; *I really had done nothing wrong!* All anyone had was just a gossip-smear campaign. Satan loves to stir gossip!

After the board meeting, eighteen people decided to gather in the church parking lot on Sunday mornings and act as negative greeters to people coming to our services. This lasted for fourteen weeks in a row. They would meet people coming to worship with the greeting, "You don't want to go in there! That man is no good! He is a thief and a liar!" After the services, these eighteen people would stand in the parking lot yelling threats at me and call me names as I locked the buildings and closed things down. They were committed to ridding the church of me as the pastor. This wasn't a pleasant time in my ministry! One by one, the congregation got discouraged and left. We'd been running nearly 200 in attendance; we dropped to less than ninety. We still had the heavy thirty-year mortgage and other regular financial obligations over our heads and only a fraction of the financial base.

Though the disgruntled people had tried everything to discourage me, nothing had made me leave my position as pastor,, so one woman told my wife, "We know how to get rid of pastors, and we will get rid of you folks too!" She leveled moral charges at me accusing me of fondling her in the church foyer. That would be completely out of character for me (I don't even like to hold hands or hug), so nobody bought in to that particular story. I'm thankful that I've been careful of improprieties throughout my ministry, or the devil would've taken that one and ran with it. I thought things couldn't get any worse. Boy, was I wrong! Satan had gotten a taste of blood and was going for the kill! I'm glad Satan can go no farther than God will allow!

Another factor causing problems was a "Christian school" the church had mothered. The school was using our building facilities and was supposed to bring financial income to help our ministry. Rather than help in the financial crisis, the school added to the crisis. What a wonderful opportunity for Satan to add fuel to an already destructive situation! The school administrator and school board wanted to add another grade to the school. This would've required another teacher, more equipment, more curriculums, and other expenses. There didn't seem to be much hope that this grade would be added to the school any time soon.

The school board asked the church board for permission to add the grade. The church board was considering the matter when the district superintendent got wind of this information and informed me that the church hadn't been able to pay its denominational budgets (general church obligations including support for missions and district church obligations including support for home missions) and we wouldn't be able to add to our ministry load until we had fulfilled our budget obligations. I told the church board what the district superintendent had ruled, and they wanted to add the grade anyway! I said, "If you go that way, you'd better get current on budgets!"

I told the district superintendent they'd decided to move ahead on the plan to expand the school. He wanted to meet with my board. The next week he met with the board—after that confrontation, they decided not to add the grade. They even decided it might be better to close the school until the church was able to get on its feet.

The next day a man came to my office whom I knew. His wife was on the school board. She was a Sunday school teacher. He also taught Sunday school. I thought he was upset and wanted to talk. I opened the door to greet him, and he slugged me in the mouth. He proceeded to beat me unmercifully and was doing a lot of damage to my physical body. He was threatening to kill me because I was planning to close the school. I tried to explain between the slugs, kicks, and gouges that he was beating the wrong fellow, but he'd have none of that. God kept telling me not to hit him back because it would make matters worse. It would've too because had I hit him, it wouldn't have been clear who'd started the conflict and who was in the wrong. Can't you imagine how Lucifer would have made hay with that!

At one point, he knocked me to the floor and proceeded to kick me in the ribs. Blood was spattered all over the floor and the walls. I knew that I had to get out of there, or he wouldn't stop until I was unconscious or dead. I headed through the door of the office and got outside to the parking lot. Some of the teachers from the school were in the parking lot, and he finally quit slugging and kicking me. He told me I'd better leave the church and the city, or he'd come back and kill me.

One of the teachers took me to a hospital emergency room for treatment. The doctor told me I was going to hurt a lot after such a severe beating. Interestingly enough, I didn't feel pain during the beating and didn't feel any pain following the beating. I never did take the pain medication the doctor had prescribed for me.

While I was in the emergency room, people were phoning each other saying that this man had come to talk to me, but I'd given a smart-aleck answer and that was why he beat me. That wasn't true! He came through the door swinging, but who wants to worry about facts when gossip is so much more interesting?

To make a long story short, another fifty people (blinded school supporters) left the church through this incident—now we were down to forty people. Forty people to carry the heavy financial load and all the expenses of running the church.

I was beat up on Wednesday. By Saturday, Satan was continuing to beat on me spiritually. During my devotions in my office (with the door locked), the devil kept saying, *What a sissy! You let somebody beat you, and you didn't lift a finger! What a wimp! Do you expect anybody to respect a chicken like you?* Isn't it strange how Satan sets things up and then accuses you like it was your fault? I was depressed and whipped!

God directed my devotional reading to Acts 5:40-41, where Peter and John were beaten by the Jewish council and instructed to speak the name of Jesus no more. They left the council "rejoicing that they were counted worthy to suffer shame for His name." I said, *God, is that what happened to me?* Suddenly, God's Holy Spirit came on me so powerfully that I spent the next forty-five minutes shouting and jumping and laughing and praising God. If you'd have come into that office, you would've thought I'd gone over the deep end and lost every bit of sense that I'd ever had.

Later that morning, I called the man who had beaten me and told him I had forgiven him for what he'd done. I asked if we could meet and pray and try to get him back in to a right relationship with Christ. He told me if I showed my face around him, he'd beat me again. I still hope and pray that he'll get things right with Jesus Christ before it's too late. I don't want Satan to win that victory.

The school finally moved out of the church facilities to another church in the city. They took most of our equipment—between $10,000 and $15,000 worth of equipment. Our church people wanted to fight, but the district superintendent instructed us not to fight. He said, "Just let it go without any more trouble. We don't need for anyone to get hurt for things that can be replaced. We don't need for things to get any worse." God didn't bless that school, and eventually they had to close their doors at the new location.

By now, the church was at the bottom. I was lower than that! I felt like I should write my name and address on the church roof in case God had forgotten where he had stuck me. My one prayer was, *God, please get me out of here!* I had now been at this church for four long miserable years!

It was time for another building payment; we hadn't recovered from the last one yet! As usual, we didn't have the money! It was a crisis! The man who held the bonds was threatening to turn the church into a skating rink. I didn't know how to get the money! I'd borrowed thousands of dollars on my personal account already in an effort to keep the church doors open. What was the use? But I couldn't give up! I'm not a quitter! The church wasn't able to pay my salary on a regular basis because of the ongoing financial crisis. I was trying to survive on credit cards.

I got sick! I ended up in the hospital with diabetes. I almost died. The doctor asked me if I'd been under any pressure. He said this diabetes was about thirty years premature. That it had been brought on by stress. I told him I couldn't imagine what would've caused that because my life was completely stressed free! Now I was also sugar free.

Thank God for a wife who would stand with me through all of that. Without her support, I would've gone under! She had her share of stress too. She is strong! I treasure her!

HOW DO DEMONS ENTER IN THE FIRST PLACE?

My oldest daughter and her family live in a relatively new neighborhood in Glendale, Arizona.

She and her husband and children were doing yard work in the front yard of their home. She and her youngest daughter were toting branches, weeds, and things that you find when you clean up a yard to the nearby trash can. Everything seemed quite tranquil and nice. My daughter noticed something that looked like a belt or a stick lying in the grass in the middle of the front yard. She went over to pick it up and throw it away with the rest of the trash. Suddenly, the thing coiled and began to make a hissing, rattling sound. It was a fairly large rattlesnake!

She knew at once that she and her family were in danger! She frantically called her husband to come destroy this poisonous rattlesnake and protect the family. He came with a shovel and began to beat and chop the snake. He managed to cut it in half, but both halves were wriggling, and the half with the head was still trying to rise up and bite him. The deadly half of the snake (the part with the head and the fangs) slithered under the bushes. Now, it had to be hunted down and finally killed, and it was going to be a whole lot harder under the shrubs. My daughter sat on the trunk of the family car and screamed in terror. My two granddaughters retreated to the front room of the house and panicked and cried hysterically because they knew daddy would be killed. My son-in-law continued to smash and chop the snake to pieces. The snake's head continued to defy death and tried to bite his assailant. Finally, the drama was played out after about twenty minutes of sheer terror. The snake was dead. The family was safe, and things could come back to normal.

Someone will say, "Well, why didn't they just leave the snake alone? It would have probably slithered away eventually! Maybe if they would have left the snake alone, it would have left them alone." Anyone knows that this isn't the answer! If you're faced with such danger, you can't just ignore it and hope that it slithers away. You must deal with the danger! Combat it until you are victorious, and your loved ones are safe.

For years I've known Christians—pastors and laypeople, who have basically held the idea that if we'll just leave Satan alone, he will leave us alone too. *Nothing could be further from the truth!* Satan is like a snake in the grass determined to destroy you, your home, your loved ones, your neighbors, and your church. We cannot just ignore him and hope he will slither away. He won't!

The Christian church has been compared to an "army marching as unto war." If this is so, then the church is the only army in the world and in history that doesn't want to know what the enemy is doing! Satan appreciates this because it makes his operation so much easier. While Christians hide their heads trying not to know what is going on around them, Satan and his demonic forces are leading a whole generation to hell!

Someone will say, "Well, I just don't believe in demons! Do you?" That's perfect reasoning for the enemy. His forces rejoice in the fact that God's people have been so blind and ignorant! While we deny him and what he is doing, he has no opposition to stop his hellish maneuvers.

I remind you that while Christ walked the earth, he believed in demonic powers. He confronted them. He battled them. He cast them out! If demons were a reality for Jesus, certainly, they are a reality for His followers today! We're living in the very last days, and demonic activity has been on the increase. Listen to what 1 Timothy 4:1-3 says: "Now the Spirit speaketh expressly, that in the latter times some shall depart from the faith, giving heed to seducing spirits, and doctrines of devils; Speaking lies in hypocrisy; having their conscience seared with a hot iron; Forbidding to marry, and commanding to abstain from meats, which God hath created to be received with thanksgiving of them which believe and know the truth."

Satan knows his time is limited, and he must do all the damage to God's kingdom while he still has time. Today there is a demonic assault on mankind unmatched in any other generation except for the generation when Jesus walked the earth. Christians are losing their homes and families to the enemy and don't even realize what is going on to cause this destruction. Parents are afraid to set down basic rules in the home for fear they might alienate the children from themselves. Churches and pastors are "watering down" God-given convictions because this generation won't tolerate the truth of God and are threatening to leave the congregations if they're made uncomfortable by the God-given conviction of sin that they feel in the service. This is the day of independent home Bible study, groups that boycott churches so people can tailor-make their religion to be just what they want it to be—tolerant of sin, nonthreatening, and comfortable.

Few people are reading God's Word. Fewer yet are praying. The home is experiencing a demonic invasion through our electronic gadgetry with the TV, VCR, DVD, Blue Ray, cell phone with all of its special features, and the home computer with its Internet connections. This doesn't even take into account the music, toys, games, and reading materials. Even the cereal boxes used at breakfast feature spooks, kooks, and demonic figures.

Even the public school system has betrayed society's trust and is now dealing with occult teachings and heathenism that does not reflect our Judeo-Christian culture.

We have so lost our moorings that the average person cannot see the harm in abortion, gay rights, or any of the other "social issues" that are destroying our homes, families, and nation today. By the way, these are not just social issues. These are "sin issues" and the "wages of sin is death" (Rom. 6:23)!

This whole generation and our children have been demonized!

If ever there was a time when God's people should wake up and pay attention to what is going on in our world, that time is today! If there ever was a time in history when a generation should be on their knees repenting and crying out to God for mercy, that time is today! But we sleep on! "Ignore it, and maybe it will go away!"

Yes, I do believe in demons! I have met several. I can honestly say, "I have never met a demon I didn't hate!" Ever since their eviction from heaven with Satan, they've been bent on destruction. Many people have demons today and will never find peace or happiness until they are set free from the demonic bondage.

"How do demons get into a person? Do they just jump in? Have I no protection?" Let's look and learn how demons enter into an individual.

There are three areas that open a person to demonic control. They are the following:

1. Inheritance
2. Occult involvement
3. Sexual sins

Ecclesiastes 10:8 says, "He that diggeth a pit shall fall into it; and whoso breaketh a hedge, a serpent shall bite him."

Most of our problems come because we've broken the protective hedge that God has placed around us. It's been broken through our own rebellion. The result has been that we have been "bitten" by a serpent (demon).

Demons cannot and do not just jump into a person uninvited. It's only as God's will (the protective hedge) is broken that we get into trouble. I call these "breaks in the hedge" or entry-point "doorways." That term isn't original with me. I picked it up from my friend, Rebecca Brown, MD, whom I admire and respect. Rebecca has written several great books on demons and spiritual warfare, and I would highly recommend that you familiarize yourself with them.

Doorway Number 1: Inheritance

Demons can enter our lives through inheritance. That is, they can pass through a family line from one generation to the next. This is in line with what the Bible has to say. In fact, Exodus, Numbers, and Deuteronomy all indicate that the sins of the parent can plague the children until the third or fourth generation (Exod. 20:5). In this case, the person didn't open the doorway, but one of his ancestors did. They were involved in some activity that opened them to demons, and the demons have remained in the family line. Now, the person who has inherited them must contend with them.

I worked with a young lady one time from Samoa. Her father had been a "medicine man" to his tribe and was known for his potent magic. He had powerful demons. He "willed" for this daughter to receive his demons at his death. He had made some pact with Satan concerning this plan. She had to disinherit these demons to be free and live for Christ.

In my own case, my great grandfather was a "medicine man" on an Indian reservation in Oklahoma. My great grandmother, his wife, was a Christian Science Practitioner. My grandmother, their daughter, was licentious. My grandfather was a Mason and a Shriner. This was all on my Dad's side of the family. This was my "heritage" coming down to me. All of the demons from my ancestors' lives were in my spiritual inheritance line. I didn't want them! I belong to Jesus Christ! (I will deal with how to rid ourselves of demons in the next chapter.)

Doorway Number 2: Occult Involvement

There shall not be found among you any one that maketh his son or his daughter to pass through the fire, or that useth divination, or an observer of times, or an enchanter, or a witch. Or a charmer, or a consulter with familiar spirits, or a wizard, or a necromancer. For all that do these things are an abomination unto the Lord:

and because of these abominations the Lord thy God doth drive them out from before thee. (Deut. 18:10-12)

Anyone who gets involved in any occult practice opens the doorway for demonic control. It's not a game and your involvement; no matter how casual is deadly! Just to be clear as to what I'm referring to, here are some examples of occult activities. This list isn't meant to be exhaustive:

Astrology
New-Age Involvement
(Eastern Religions
Horoscopes
Ouija Board
Fortune-teller
Palm Reader
Drugs (anything going for a high outside the will of God)
Alcohol
Hypnosis
Occult healings
Transcendental meditation
Yoga
Occult movies
Belief in reincarnation
Secret, Oath-bound Societies
(Masons, Rosicrucians, etc.)
Oaths and Pledges Taken Through College Sororities and Fraternities

Reading Books on "Occult Arts"

Psychic experiences
Astral Projection
Martial Arts
Meditation (blanking the mind)
Witchcraft (either white or black)
Dungeons and Dragons (and other role-playing games)
Visualization and Guided imagery
Biofeedback
Séance
Rock Music
Acupuncture
Spirit Guides
Blasphemy
Silva Mind Control
Self-hypnosis

The list could go on for quite a while, but I want to point out various ways in which Satan is working today to infest our society with demonic control. Our communication airways are flooded with occult trash. Our homes are being invaded through television and radio. The cartoons our children watch today are largely occult in nature. They're no longer designed to be funny—now they teach witchcraft to our children. All these modes of modern entertainment and communication give Satan free access to our homes and our minds. We need to pray for wisdom and for the ability to turn destructive programs off rather than to let them come into our living rooms. They're dulling our moral senses to the point that we no longer know right from wrong!

Our public school system is saturated with New Age teachings and techniques. The "outcome-based education" is being pushed on our children today and is designed to do away with morals, patriotism, and Christian ethics that we want our children to have. I plan to deal with this matter in a later book.

Christians! It's time to wake up to the times in which we are living and to sharpen our commitments to Jesus Christ!

Doorway Number 3: Sexual Sins

God's purpose for instructing us to abstain from fornication and fleshly lusts, which war against the soul (Acts 15:20, 1 Thess. 4:3, and 1 Pet. 2:11) wasn't to be a cosmic killjoy trying to destroy all of our fun and pleasure. His purpose was to protect us from disease and demonic entry! *Sexual sins are open doorways for demons!*

First Corinthians 6:18, "Flee fornication. Every sin that a man doeth is without the body; but he that committeth fornication sinneth against his own body!"

If a person has a sexual relationship outside the protective bonds of marriage (the "marriage bed"), he has opened himself up to every demon that his sexual partner has, and the partner is open to every demon that he has. *Condoms will not protect us from demons either!* The only way that a person can protect himself/herself from demonic entry, disease, pregnancy, and guilt is to follow God's design and marry his lover and keep himself faithful and pure!

> Marriage is honorable in all, and the bed undefiled: but whoremongers and adulterers God will judge. (Heb. 13:4)

This sexually promiscuous generation has certainly enabled satanic forces to have free hand in our society! People have lost their morals and values and have treated God's guidelines with contempt. Man cannot ignore and break God's laws without paying a heavy price. I believe AIDS and other sexually transmitted diseases are certainly part of the price being paid for our sexual rebellion. One day God will further judge mankind for sin and "the wicked shall be turned into hell, and all the nations that forget God (Ps. 9:17).

Fornication, adultery, homosexuality, any form of sexual perversion, pornography, incest, molestation, rape, masturbation, sadomasochism, sexual counseling from the opposite sex, sex with animals, and any other sexual perversion will open doors to demonic infestation.

There seems to be a lot of confusion in our generation in regard to what is termed "the homosexual lifestyle." *It is sin!* It isn't a sexual orientation or sexual preference or an alternate lifestyle. *It is sin!* "Gays" and "lesbians" as they are called are not a minority group, which should be given special rights. *They are sinners!* By the way, *gay* is a misnomer. The people caught up in that life are not happy but are miserable and trapped!

Quickly, I need to say that homosexuality indeed *is a sin*, and people who practice this activity are indeed *sinners*, but God still loves them. God hates the sin (all sin) but loves the sinner and God can forgive the sin and cleanse the sinner if confession and repentance is made.

> If we confess our sins, He is faithful and just to forgive us our sins,
> and to cleanse us from all unrighteousness. (1 John 1:9)

Jesus Christ became the very essence of sin, died on the cross, went to hell, and rose again the third day in order to forgive sin. Homosexuality can be forgiven just like any other sin. The homosexual needs to get off the defensive about his sin and forsake it just like any other sin.

> For God sent not His Son to condemn the world; but that the
> world through Him might be saved. (John 3:17)

> The promise is true for this sin too: "The blood of Jesus Christ
> his Son cleanseth us from all sin. (1 John 1:7b)

It's been my experience that the gays and lesbians that I've worked with have at one time been sexually molested, and this experience has opened the door to Satan's demons. Usually, the victim has to release the person who molested them to Jesus Christ and has to forgive that one for the terrible deed that was done.

We can't do this in our own power. It takes the help of God to take such action. After the step of forgiveness has been accomplished, the one who is seeking deliverance then asks for forgiveness for his own perverted sin. Christ's blood can cleanse from *all sins*, and when Jesus is asked sincerely with repentance, He will cleanse away this sin too.

Now, the person addresses the demons that have come in through these experiences and commands them to leave in the name of Jesus Christ.

It's possible for the person to do this now because Satan no longer has legal ground to stay in a life that has been forgiven and cleansed by God through the blood of Christ.

Remember, no matter how a demon has gained access to your being, he has no legal authority to stay there when you accept Christ's cleansing and become a child of God.

HOW TO BE SET FREE!

If the Son, therefore, shall make you free, ye shall be free indeed.

—John 8:36

He that diggeth a pit shall fall into it; and whoso breaketh a hedge, a serpent shall bite him.

—Ecclesiastes 10:8

What if I'm a victim? How do I get Satan and his filthy demons out of my life? How can I be set free? These questions are extremely important to someone who feels he's opened doorways (broken a hedge) and is in spiritual bondage to Satan and his destructive forces.

People have come to me from all over the United States and Canada wanting to be free. They've been enslaved to sin and feel hopelessly trapped in their situations. *Good news!* Satan can't put anything so deep into the human heart, but the blood of Jesus Christ can cleanse even deeper!

Satan *cannot* get such a hold upon your life that Christ cannot set you free if you really want to be free! Jesus Christ paid the price to free us from *all* sin! What you've done in the past may bring you pain, embarrassment, and shame, but God can restore you to a right relationship with Him as one of His children adopted into His family. You must seek His forgiveness and power with true repentance.

What is repentance? It's more than just being sorry you were caught or got into trouble. *Repentance is a personal sorrow for sin. It involves true confession, the asking for forgiveness, a turning away from sinful activity, and a personal resolve to change life's direction.* It's not trying to excuse or explain away sin. It is *stopping* (quitting) the sin activity that got you into trouble in the first place. It is walking a new life with Christ Jesus!

The Apostle Paul said, "Therefore if any man be in Christ, he is a new creature: old things are passed away; behold, all things are become new (2 Cor. 5:17).

Too many people are willing to settle for a "mind change" where they give mental assent to the fact that Christ is the Son of God and that He really did die for sin. What is needed is more than just facts. What is needed is a heart change and a relationship with Jesus Christ as Savior and Lord. One needs to be willing to "deny himself and take up his cross and follow" Jesus (Matt. 16:24).

Once a person has really repented and turned from sin, he's in a position to "boot" Satan and his demons out of his life if there's been any problem with demonic bondage. It does no good and probably much harm to try to guide a non-Christian through a deliverance experience. He has no legal ground to maintain his spiritual freedom. The demons may be commanded away in the name of Jesus Christ and will have left in obedience to a Christian's authority in Christ Jesus, but a sinner has no way to keep them from returning later. Remember, when a demon returns, he brings up to seven of his friends with him and the condition of the sinner is much worse than he was before. Matthew 12:43-45: "(Jesus said) When the unclean spirit is gone out of a man, he walketh through dry places, seeking rest, and findeth none. Then he saith, I will return into my house from whence I came out; and when he is come, he findeth it empty, swept, and garnished. Then goeth he, and taketh seven other spirits more wicked than himself, and they enter in and dwell there: and the last state of that man is worse than the first."

Once it's been established that the person is genuinely "saved," he can begin evicting the demons that have been harassing him. Usually, someone will ask, "Well, can't you just cast them out? Why make the person with the problem get involved?" Who let them in there in the first place? He is involved!

The answer is, "Yes, I, as a Christian, do have Christ's authority available to me through the blood and resurrection. I can cast demons out, but the person needs to learn to fight for himself. He needs to realize his own authority in Christ." If demons harass him and I'm not there to help, he could panic unless he knows how to do battle for himself. It's Christ's authority and not mine that makes the demons flee. Each Christian has access to that authority for himself. We're responsible to use the power and authority given us through Christ and clear the demons out of our own lives. Jesus said, "Behold, I give unto you power to tread on serpents and scorpions, and over all the power of the enemy: and nothing shall by any means hurt you. Notwithstanding in this rejoice not, that the spirits are subject unto you; but rather rejoice, because your names are written in Heaven (Luke 10:19-20).

> Submit yourselves therefore to God. Resist the devil, and he will
> flee from you. (James 4:7)

I ask the person wanting deliverance to make a list of possible doorways (holes in the hedge) that have allowed demonic entrance. He is to categorize the three main areas of demonic entry. *Inheritance, occult involvement,* and *sexual encounters.* He is to list the doorways in each category. This should be done with much prayer seeking God's help and guidance. After the list has been made, I sit down with the person and look over what has been remembered. Often, God will guide me to ask about something that may be related to the listed doorways, but has been forgotten by the person. We then proceed to go down the list, and the person confesses each sin and asks for forgiveness and cleansing for each one. As the confession is made of each sin, Satan and his demons are addressed and commanded to leave in the *name of Jesus Christ.* The door is then closed and covered with the blood of Christ, and that person is free from the demon that entered into his life through that sin.

One of the first things I do in a deliverance is to find if the person can see into the spirit world—that is, see demons. We're not supposed to be able to see into the spirit world unless God gives us that special privilege on very rare occasions (2 Kings 6:17). Most of the time we are to "walk by faith, not by sight" (2 Cor. 5:7).

To understand what I'm trying to explain, we need to comprehend the makeup of man. Most people just see the physical body and think that is all there is. We're made up of three parts: body, soul, and spirit. The body is the container or "space suit," which makes it possible for the soul and spirit of man to survive here on earth. The body is the part of man that dies and decays in the grave. At the first resurrection or the resurrection of the saints, we will be given a new or glorified body that will be indestructible and eternal. Our body will be like Christ's body after the resurrection. It'll not be subject to aging, sickness, or death. It will be indestructible so that our enjoyment of heaven will be enhanced. Interestingly enough, those who will be a part of the second resurrection, the resurrection of the damned, will also have a glorified body that cannot be destroyed. This will enhance the torment of hell.

The soul is the seat of natural life, where the natural faculties of the conscious man dwell. "It is the intermediary between the body and the spirit, the seat of personality."[1] The soul is eternal and doesn't die when the body dies.

---

[1]   W.T. Purkiser, Ph.D., editor, *Exploring Our Christian Faith* (1960) Beacon Hill Press of Kansas City, p. 210

"The spirit is declared to be the organ of divine life and communion with God, the seat of divine indwelling."[2] The spirit is the part of us that's created in the likeness of God. It's the spirit that recognizes guilt and conviction. The spirit is what affects us when we complain that our conscience is hurting us. The spirit doesn't die.

"It is well to remember that body, soul, and spirit are so united as to form one integrated personality."[3]

"It should be noted that, while man shares spirit with God, he shares soul with the animals (Gen. 1:21 and 24, where "creature" translates *nephesh* and Rev. 16:3). Generally speaking, soul is attributed to man and to animals, not to God. On the other hand, spirit is attributed to God and to man, not to animals."[4]

Look at some scripture references, which support this truth:

> And the very God of peace sanctify you wholly; and I pray God
> your whole spirit and soul and body be preserved blameless unto
> the coming of our Lord Jesus Christ. (1 Thess. 5:23)

Paul is teaching us that the human is a trichotomous being. That is three parts—body, soul, and spirit. He says all three must be cleansed and committed to Christ. Jesus, Himself, must help us to keep all three parts "blameless" until His coming again.

> And the Lord God formed man of the dust of the ground and
> breathed into his nostrils the breath of life; and man became a
> living soul. (Gen. 2:7)

"That is, Adam lived, and became aware of himself. In essence our self is our soul, which manifests as our mind, our will, and our emotions."[5]

> It is sown a natural body; it is raised a spiritual body. There is a
> natural body, and there is a spiritual body. (1 Cor. 15:44)

---

2   Ibid., p. 210
3   Ibid., p. 210
4   Ibid., p. 218
5   Rebecca Brown, M.D., *Prepare For War*, (1987), Chick Publications, p. 244

"Our spirits have a form or shape, a body corresponding to our physical body. Few people other than the Satanists, or those involved in such things as astral projection, realize this."[6] The spiritual body is attached to the physical body by a silver cord. If that silver cord is broken, the body dies.

> Or ever the silver cord be loosed, or the golden bowl be broken, or the pitcher be broken at the fountain, or the wheel broken at the cistern. Then shall the dust return to the earth as it was: and the spirit shall return unto God who gave it. (Eccles. 12:6-7)

I've worked with some who have claimed to have experienced astral projections (had out-of-body experiences). They've told me they were aware of the silver cord attaching their spirit to their body. They also knew that if it were broken, they would instantly die. Several scriptures deal with out-of-body experiences:

> James 2:26 reminds us, "For as the body without the spirit is dead . . ." Once the spirit is no longer attached to the body, death occurs instantly.

> I knew a man in Christ above fourteen years ago, (whether in the body, I cannot tell; or whether out of the body, I cannot tell; God knoweth:) such an one caught up to the third heaven. And I knew such a man, (whether in the body, or out of the body, I cannot tell: God knoweth:) How that he was caught up into paradise, and heard unspeakable words, which it is not lawful for a man to utter. (2 Cor. 12:2-4)

> After this I looked, and, behold, a door was opened in Heaven: and the first voice which I heard was as it were a of a trumpet talking with me; which said, come up hither, and I will shew thee things which must be hereafter. And immediately I was in the spirit: and, behold, a throne was set in Heaven, and one sat on the throne. (Rev. 4:1-2)

Now, we go one step further in this attempt to understand how a person could see into the spiritual world.

---

[6]   Ibid., p. 244

> For the Word of God is quick, and powerful, and sharper than a
> two-edged sword, piercing even the dividing asunder of soul and
> spirit . . . (Heb. 4:12)

The question comes, why is it necessary to divide between our soul and our spirit? That is what Hebrews 4:12 is saying, that there can be a division made (or separation of) the soul and the spirit.

When Adam and Eve were created, before they sinned, they could see into the spirit world as readily as they could see the physical world. They did this by using their spiritual bodies. That's why it was easy for them to walk and talk with God in the Garden of Eden. They were as aware of their spiritual bodies as they were of their physical bodies. When they sinned (rebelled against God and fell from grace), spiritual death took place. They were no longer "consciously aware of their spiritual bodies, and thus could not commune with the Lord as they had once done."[7]

There was a link between spirit and soul, which allowed man to see the spirit world. When Adam and Eve sinned, God severed that link, stopping man's awareness of the spiritual world. God doesn't want us to see or contact the spirit world.

"Clearly, it is NOT the Lord's will for His people to have this control over their spirits. Our spirits are to be directly under the control of the Holy Spirit, NOT our minds."[8]

"This is the basic difference between the occult and Christianity. Occultists control their contact with the spirit world, and they control, to a large extent, the power they use. Christians, on the other hand, are never in contact with the spirit world except on the brief occasions the Holy Spirit allows such contact, and Christians do NOT control the power of their God in any way. Christians are servants, nothing more. The Lord works through his servants as *he* chooses, not as they choose. Demons cooperate with humans to give them power when the people want it to draw them ever farther away from the Lord."[9]

There are certain demons Satan uses to build a corrupt link in fallen man so he can see and contact the spirit world. These are called "power demons," and they help a person gain conscious control of his spirit.[10] The

---

[7]   Ibid., p. 246

[8]   Rebecca Brown, M.D., *Becoming a Vessel of Honor* (1990), Whitaker House, p. 170

[9]   Ibid., p. 170

[10]   Rebecca Brown M.D., *Prepare for War*, p. 250

imagination and visualization are key factors in building the link between the soul and spirit. It's often overlooked as a source of torment and trouble in a deliverance. If this demonic link between soul and spirit is left unsevered, the person who has been involved in the occult is open to constant demonic harassment and torment from Satan's kingdom.

Therefore, one of the first things I do in a deliverance is to have the person repent for his ability to see into the spirit world. He must renounce that power and ask God to sever that demonic link. Then he must rebuke and bind those power demons and send them on their way in the *name of Jesus Christ*. Once this has been accomplished, the person will no longer be able to see the spirit world. He now has to move by faith just like the rest of us.

Then we proceed as I started to describe several paragraphs back. The person first deals with the *lines of inheritance*. He renounces any demonic inheritance from his family and asks God to break those inheritance lines that come down to him. He then rebukes, binds, and commands the demons that have come to him through inheritance to leave in the *name of Jesus*. It's important to remember we are using Christ's power and that we have no authority or power in our own strength.

I've heard people say, "Satan, I rebuke you," or "Satan, I come against you." I'm sure Satan must say, "Big deal! Who are you and what power do you think that you have?" *Our power and strength comes through Jesus Christ. We must remember to identify where our authority comes from. That's the only thing demons and Satan understand! By the same token, we must be in an up-to-date close relationship with Jesus Christ, or we might get hurt badly!*

You probably remember the story of the seven sons of Sceva in Acts 19:13-16. These men didn't have a personal relationship with Jesus Christ. They tried to cast a demon out of an individual and demanded that the demon leave by saying, "We adjure you by Jesus whom Paul preacheth." The demon answered, "Jesus I know, and Paul I know, but who are you?" With that, the man with the demon in him jumped on them and beat them all soundly.

After the demon has been told to leave, I have the person close that door and cover it with the *blood of Jesus Christ*!

We continue on working through the areas of the occult and sexual sins. Each doorway is recognized and confessed to Jesus Christ each time the person asks for and accepts Christ's forgiveness for those sins. When confession is made and forgiveness is asked for and received, the person addresses the demons that have entered through that doorway and commands them to leave in the name of Jesus Christ. That particular door is closed and covered by the blood of Jesus Christ. The person must realize that he is being cleansed and set free.

> If we confess our sins, he is faithful and just to forgive us our sins, and to cleanse us from all unrighteousness. (1 John 1:9)

What a wonderful thing for the person to finally be set free!

> If the Son, therefore, shall make you free, ye shall be free indeed. (John 8:36)

After every sin has been confessed and every door closed, I ask the person to dedicate himself completely to God. I pray for him and ask God to completely cleanse the body, soul, and spirit and accept this person as a "living sacrifice, holy acceptable unto God" (Rom. 12:1-2).

Finally, I anoint the person with oil in the name of the Father, Son, and Holy Spirit and pray with him that he'll choose to remain faithful to God. He asks the Holy Spirit to fill the void that is left in his life.

Some ask me, "Is it necessary to identify every doorway that we have and confess each sin?" I believe it's extremely important to do this. I've seen deliverances where the person has hidden some pet sin that he didn't want to confess or stop doing. This has left an open doorway and an invitation to the demons to come pouring back in to this life. When this happens the, torment the person experiences increases and gets much worse. We must give ourselves to God 100 percent! If we haven't given Him our all, we have given Him nothing at all! God is not interested in just playing around with us, and neither is Satan. The stakes are eternal!

If nothing else is accomplished when the person confesses every doorway and repents for every sin, at least he hasn't taken the act of repentance lightly! He knows that all sins have been confessed to Jesus. Should Satan ever try to challenge and accuse him of past sins, he can know the problem has been dealt with, and he doesn't have to listen to Satan's tormenting lies! God has cleansed him from all those sins just as He promised He would do. Satan might remember what happened long ago, but God has removed that sin as far as the east is from the west! Check out Psalm 103:12.

Finally, I give the person scripture-memorization assignments, remind him to be faithful in his prayer and Bible reading, and tell him to be certain he obeys God at every point. Fill the void with God, God's Word, and obedience to God's will!

I admonish the person not to reopen any doors. He doesn't want those demons coming back in, each bringing "seven of his friends."

Often, I'm asked if I worry about demonic manifestations during a deliverance session. "What if a demon would manifest?"

The person going through the deliverance can control that situation for the most part. There is no reason for a demon to take over the deliverance! We are created free-moral individuals with power of choice, and the person can choose not to let the demon manifest. God will give the person power and authority to "rebuke and bind" the demon in the name of Jesus Christ. I always warn the person that if he decides not to control the demon himself that I'll stand back and let the demon deal with him as the demon sees fit.

On occasion, I've had a demon render a person unconscious. At that point, I anoint the person with oil and command the demon to release the person (again, using the name of Jesus Christ). I always keep myself alert to what's happening around me during a deliverance. Usually I have one or two other trusted prayer warriors there to give prayer support and to lend spiritual power when needed. I insist that one of the three keep his eyes open at all times. I generally try to remember to keep my eyes open too, but once in awhile forget and shut them because I'm in a prayer mode. Someone must be seeing what is going on, to be aware if the demon begins to manifest or cause the person to become violent.

I worked with one young man in Phoenix, who I will call Barry (not his real name). Barry had become infested with demons. He had done drugs, been involved in the occult, been a male prostitute, had frequent and varied sexual experiences (most of them totally perverted!), and had opened himself up to Satan in several other ways. While counseling with Barry, he would often go into a trance and quit responding to the conversation. I'd see in his eyes a demon mocking and laughing at me. I would rebuke that demon in the name of Jesus and command that he would let me talk to Barry without his interference. At this point, Barry would snap out of the trance and begin to respond in the conversation again.

I told Barry at the time of his deliverance that he would have to control that demon. As we prayed, he went unconscious. I anointed him and commanded the demon, in the name of Jesus, to stop doing that! Suddenly, I heard a low guttural voice say, "You can't have him he is mine! I have a right to him!" I looked up and Barry (who weighed less than 120 pounds), had the heavy altar rail poised above his head ready to smash it down on top of me. I saw the evil demon in his eyes again radiating hatred at me. My prayer partners began to pray in earnest and I, in Jesus's name, commanded

Barry to put the altar down on the floor again where it belonged. Again, I rebuked the demon in the name of Jesus and told him that Barry did not belong to him but had been purchased by the atoning blood of Jesus Christ and was Christ's property. I further threatened that if the demon caused more trouble, I'd petition God to send him to the pit early, before his time. The demon backed off. I told Barry we'd have no more scenes like that one and that he'd better take control of the situation or we would stop the deliverance right then and there! Barry did take control. He was set free that night and is still maintaining a walk with Jesus Christ today.

I've known well-meaning pastors and people who think you have to know a demon's name before you can cast him out. That's just not true!

If we are contending with a spirit guide and the person does know a name for this demon, I'll certainly address that demon by name and dismiss him in the name of Jesus Christ.

For the most part, it isn't necessary to identify a demon by name. They're all liars and will not tell you their true name anyway. I don't argue with demons! I don't reason with demons! I don't care to know who they are or anything about their history. We're not to communicate with the spirit world by order of God. If we do, we sin. Therefore, I command them to get out in the name of Jesus! You wouldn't try to find out a name of a snake, rat, or mouse that you were trying to evict from your house. You probably wouldn't even care about its personal history. They're just vermin and filth that needs to be destroyed. So are demons!

Again, when a person has been set free from demonic infestation, there is a void that is left. That emptiness had better be filled by the Holy Spirit and the things of God, or Satan will return and try to reclaim the property that used to be his. Get the person in to the Word of God. Teach him to pray. Teach him to obey God. Be ready to stand with him and help nurture him to maturity.

HOW TO STAY FREE FROM DEMONIC BONDAGE

Satan doesn't like to lose anyone whom he considers his property. He'll do everything he can to contest the victory of the deliverance and try to win back that which he's lost. It's extremely important for the person who has been delivered to safeguard his life against Satan and his demons.

Jesus Christ warned about this in the Gospels of Matthew and Luke.

> When the unclean spirit is gone out of a man, he walketh through dry places, seeking rest; and finding none, he saith, I will return unto my house from whence I came out. And when he cometh, he findeth it swept and garnished. Then goeth he, and taketh to him seven other spirits more wicked than himself; and they enter in, and dwell there: and the last state of that man is worse than the first. (Luke 11:24-26)

The words of Jesus are almost identical with those previously quoted in Matthew 12:43-45.

After a person has evicted the demonic entities that had been controlling him, he is now empty and has a spiritual void. This void must be filled with something. Either the person will fill the void with things of God and victory, or the demon will return with friends and fill that void with evil and defeat. It's important that the person begins immediately to read his Bible, pray, and memorize scripture. He must decide to live a life of complete obedience to God and give God's Holy Spirit access to every part of his life. When one is filled and controlled by the Holy Spirit, Satan can't work his way back in to control.

HOW TO OVERCOME TEMPTATION

He will still be subject to temptation. Too many people think that Christians aren't tempted. Nothing is further from the truth. A Christian still has choice and can choose to follow Christ's will or reject Christ's will. This is called being a "free-moral agent." If Satan can get a person to choose against Christ and rebel against God, he'll have a point of entry to get back into that life bringing more defeat and spiritual agony. For this reason, Satan and his demons will see that we're tempted to disobey God. Don't be afraid! God has promised victory if we want victory. Listen to God's Word:

> There hath no temptation taken you but such as is common to man: but God is faithful, who will not suffer you to be tempted above that ye are able; but will with the temptation also make a way to escape, that ye may be able to bear it. (1 Cor. 10:13)

There's a difference between temptation and sin. We will all be tempted, but we don't have to sin. Temptation says, "Will you?" Sin says, "I will!" Sin comes when we put our desires and self ahead of God. A good definition of sin is, *sin is selfishness!* All Satan did when he brought sin into God's universe was to exalt himself above God's will.

That's the same thing that happened in Eden: Adam and Eve overrode God's will by doing their own selfish wills.

How can a Christian handle temptation? Satan will constantly bombard him with temptation. He and his demons will be putting thoughts into his head at every opportunity.

My grandmother used to tell me, "You can't stop the crows from flying over your head, but you don't have to let them nest in your hair."

A Christian can't stop Satan from firing thoughts of temptation at his mind, but he doesn't have to give them a place to lodge and roost. When temptation comes, the Christian has the freedom to choose to dwell on that thought or to put it out of his thinking.

Jesus handled Satan's temptations by quoting God's Word back to the devil. I can use God's Word the very same way! "Thy Word have I hid in my heart, that I might not sin against thee" (Ps. 119:11). Satan can't contend with God's Word. It'll defeat him every time!

That's why it's important after a person is freed from demonic bondage to begin reading and memorizing scripture. Let God's Word cleanse and fortify your being. A Christian can't be easily led astray when he knows what God's Word says!

Another important step to staying free from demonic bondage is to develop an active prayer life. As a Christian prays, his walk with God is strengthened. The child of God understands more about God and His will because he's gotten personally acquainted with God. As he prays, God will reveal His plan for his life. A Christian must commit himself to being obedient to God's will. When we're obeying God, we don't have time to fall into sin.

If a person does slip and yield to a temptation, he needs to come to God and ask for God's forgiveness. He can then go on from there in his Christian journey. Remember 1 John 1:9, reminds us "If we confess our sins, He is faithful and just to forgive us our sins, and to cleanse us from all unrighteousness."

Too often, people teach that if you've yielded to temptation and let sin come into your life, you must go back to the very beginning of your walk with Christ and start all over again. If you fall off a bicycle, you don't go back to where you started. You pick yourself up, dust yourself off, and go on from there. If we Christians fall, we do the same thing. We pick ourselves up, straighten things out with God, and go from there. The secret is to not wait for a long time after the fall to come back to God but to come to Him immediately. God wants to restore you to Himself. God wants you to have victory! He wants you to get to heaven even more than you want to get there! This doesn't mean God is soft on sin! This means God loves you and will sustain you if you want to do His will.

> The Lord is not slack concerning His promise, as some men count slackness; but is long-suffering to us-ward, not willing that any should perish, but that all should come to repentance. (2 Pet. 3:9)

God will stand with you and strengthen you as you decide to walk with Him!

After a deliverance from satanic bondage, it's necessary to clean out our home. There'll be items that will not be to the glory of God. There will be things that, if left there, will cause failure and defeat because they'll give Satan legal access to your living area. Such things as tapes, records, CDs, DVDs, movies, books, magazines, computer games and software, souvenirs, idols, alcohol, cigarettes, drugs, toys, rosaries, Masonic items, and etc. Things that God can't be glorified with must be destroyed. Your home now must be God-controlled and God-centered.

The old lifestyle and habits will have to be modified to reflect your obedience to God. Old habits that brought defeat in the past must be surrendered to God for His guidance and control. There might even be some changes in friendships if your present friends drag you away from God's will.

This sounds hard—maybe even impossible. The good news is God will direct you and use you and make it easier for you as He fills the void that's been left in your spiritual life. He'll fill that void with Himself! God never asks a person to give up anything without replacing that thing with something better!

His cleansing brings joy, peace, and contentment that's not possible from any other source. Let God have complete control of your life today!

I'd suggest you learn to anoint your home with oil as you consecrate it to Jesus Christ. The anointing of oil is discussed in the chapter in this book entitled Anointing with Oil.

In summary, after a person has been cleansed from demonic control, he needs to fill that void with God. He needs to do everything he can to allow God's presence in his life. As he reads God's Word, spends time in prayer and communion with God, obeys God's will, attends church services (this must be a Godly church preaching the truths of God), witnesses to others, and develops good habits of stewardship to God, he should be so saturated with God that the devil won't be able to get another foothold in his life. Remember, Satan can only defeat us when we're willing to cooperate with him and disobey our Savior, Jesus Christ!

LEST YE FALL

An area needing a word of caution today is the area of counseling. Too many pastors and dedicated Christians feel their particular strength lies in this area, and they love to speak and hear themselves talk. I'm not saying that sound counseling isn't important, but I am saying we must be extremely careful. Any counsel offered must be steeped in prayer and rooted deeply in the Word of God.

Often, this aspect of the ministry becomes an area of pride. A pastor can be overly impressed with his own wisdom, insights, and abilities and forget that any wisdom he might demonstrate comes from God. Satan watches for an arrogant attitude with relish and delights in setting such a person up for defeat! Too many pastors feel they're no longer vulnerable to Satan and temptation. Nothing's farther from the truth! Satan will do all he can to help a Christian fall, especially a church leader.

When I was in Phoenix, Arizona, I met an ex-witch who is now a Christian. She had come to one of our seminars on spiritual warfare. She caught me between sessions and said, "You don't remember me, do you?" I had to admit that I didn't. She told me she'd been in my church in Cheyenne, Wyoming. She'd belonged to a coven in Longmont, Colorado, and had been sent to my church with the expressed purpose of causing me to fall morally, thus destroying my ministry. She said she'd attended my church on four consecutive Sundays but couldn't get me to pay any attention to her flirtatious ways. Finally, she concluded that I was happily married and probably wouldn't compromise myself to the temptation she was prepared to offer. I'm pleased that I've always tried to be cautious and discreet in my dealings with ladies. I knew one pastor who would have long counseling sessions with women in the church. Sessions that would last hours at a time. He'd even go to their home to counsel with them. I don't know anything indiscreet happened, but I do know he was setting himself up for disaster. If some lady wanted to make accusations and press charges or if her husband became jealous, the pastor would've been in a precarious position.

Ministers have to realize that we're special targets of the enemy! Even though we feel that everything is under control and is right and proper, we must "avoid the very appearance of evil." My heart was broken recently as I received word that one of my pastor friends that I've known and respected for years was caught in a compromising situation and had to surrender his credentials. I can't stress loud or long enough how careful a man or woman of God has to be in this day in which we live. Satan is looking for a way to bring us down! We'd better not give him ammunition!

A pretty young woman came to me in Phoenix, Arizona. She wanted me to train her in spiritual warfare. She'd heard that I had experience in this area and wanted to learn from a veteran. She explained she was dating a man whom she thought would become a pastor and probably get active in warfare ministry. She wanted to understand as much as she could "so she could be a better wife for him." I told her she should speak to my wife because she knew more about the role the girl would play as a minister's wife. She didn't want to speak to my wife but would rather learn things from my perspective. She suggested that I reserve time each week we could meet together uninterrupted, and I could "train her." Red flags were flying all over this situation. The temptation was to ignore them and see what she had in mind, but my walk with God and my love for my wife and my ministry are too important to do anything so flippant. I told her, "No! Either you be satisfied with meeting with my wife, or forget the whole information thing!" Too many times, our inflated egos suck us into dangerous situations! We must be careful! There's too much at stake to make a big mistake!

I don't have a counseling session with any lady unless someone, my wife or a secretary, is in the *near* vicinity. I limit my counseling time to one hour or less. I'm careful about any physical contact (I don't hug or hold hands and pray). I'm careful about any intimate conversation or flirtatious remarks. I don't counsel a woman about sexual matters unless my wife or her husband is in the room. If the counseling requires more than three or four sessions, I refer the lady to a Christian counselor who is trained in such matters.

I've been accused of being too silly in these matters. One time a woman accused me of a moral compromise with her, but nobody believed her accusations because I've been consistent in these guidelines. A man who won't even hug isn't going to do the things this woman was implying that I had done.

I've seen well-meaning, innocent pastors wanting to hug all over their parishioners. I warned one man that this isn't a good practice. He said, "Well, that's just the way that I am. I'm not a cold fish like you!" Maybe a man should pray that God will help him to be a little more like a "cold fish." It might be what he needs to keep him out of hot water.

Scripture gives clear guidelines concerning a Christian's conduct. If we follow the scriptural admonitions, we should live above reproach. Listen to God's Word:

> Abstain from all appearance of evil. (1 Thess. 5:22)

> Ye therefore, beloved, seeing ye know these things before, beware lest ye also, being led away with the error of the wicked, fall from your own stedfastness. (2 Pet. 3:17)

> Be sober, be vigilant; because your adversary the devil, as a roaring lion, walketh about, seeking whom he may devour: Whom resist stedfast in the faith, knowing that the same afflictions are accomplished in your brethren that are in the world. (1 Pet. 5:8-9)

> There hath no temptation taken you but such as is common to man: but God is faithful, who will not suffer you to be tempted above that ye are able; but will with the temptation also make a way of escape, that ye may be able to bear it. (1 Cor. 10:13)

I'm informed there exists coven-training programs to teach attractive young women how to trap and bring a minister down morally. The women are sent out to churches with this purpose in mind. If Satan can "ruin" a pastor, he's scored a major victory against God.

Certainly, if a pastor is walking daily with the Lord, if he's in the Bible each day, and if he is praying diligently and keeping up-to-date in his relationship with Jesus Christ and being obedient to Christ, he'll not be brought down morally. It's when we get too proud and important and we don't act cautiously and discreetly that we get into trouble. God help us to keep our eyes on the goal and not allow Satan the liberty to destroy our ministry!

Sexual immorality isn't the only pitfall a Christian must watch for in his or her ministry. Satan can hit us through improper reading or television, or conversations or attitudes or a multitude of other things he has in his arsenal. In a neighboring town, a well-known and respected pastor in a strong church setting let his guard down and has marred if not destroyed his ministry. He became enamored with the computer. He wouldn't go anywhere without his laptop computer. It had become an obsession with him. He was continuously online and enjoyed communicating with other computer lovers. One day, he made contact with a girlfriend he knew before he was married to his present wife. He began corresponding online with this lady. The communication became more and more frequent until he was so preoccupied with this relationship that he neglected his wife, his family, his church, and God. His sermons showed lack of preparation. He lost interest in his congregation. He began having marital problems. Finally, the situation was discovered and brought to the open. He was asked to resign from his church. How subtle Satan can be, and how destructive are his ways!

One thing I ask myself for any and every activity is this: "would Christ do this with me?" If not, I shouldn't do it either.

When I watch TV, I ask if Christ would watch this program with me. When I read or converse or attend certain gatherings or any activity I'm doing, I should be conscious as to whether Christ would enjoy this with me—the truth is He is with me as I do the activity and if He doesn't approve I'll find it out now or later, but I will learn His opinion.

The Christian needs to "put on the whole armor of God, that ye may be able to stand against the wiles of the devil" (Eph. 6:11-18). It would be well to commit that passage to memory. Most folks don't understand this is literal spiritual armor. It isn't just symbolism. We need to have God dress us in our armor each day. We need to realize Satan is going to attack, and we need to be prepared to stand victoriously!

The only reason for casualties on the battlefield of spiritual warfare is that we get our eyes off Christ and compromise our convictions. We need to join Paul the Apostle in 2 Timothy 1:12, "For the which cause I also suffer these things: nevertheless I am not ashamed: for I know whom I have believed, and am persuaded that He is able to keep that which I have committed unto Him against that day."

In all the talk about Satan and demons and spiritual warfare, don't forget that Satan is just minor league compared to our God! Jesus is faithful! He's more powerful than Satan—one day Satan will bow before Jesus and confess Him as Lord. "That at the name of Jesus every knee shall bow . . . and that every tongue should confess that Jesus Christ is Lord, to the glory of God the Father" (Phil. 2:10-11).

The Bible teaches that the day is coming when Satan will be cast into the lake of fire (Rev. 20:10) where he'll not bother us ever again. I want to be on the lakeshore that day leading the cheering section as we see our archenemy get his just deserts.

We must remember, Jesus Christ has promised never to leave us or forsake us! With His help, we can remain faithful and victorious! *Praise God!*

CHURCH INFILTRATORS

Satan doesn't want God's church to succeed! He'll do whatever it takes to ensure that your church and your ministry is destroyed. Naturally, Satan realizes that he can't send obvious Satanists into your church because you would know to be on your guard against such people. The Devil is a master of deceit—he passes himself off as an "angel of light." He often comes as a concerned "friend" to give you aid and support in your ministry. His infiltrators are no different. Usually, they seem like "godsend" when they show up at the church. But too many times, you'll find the god they serve isn't our Lord and Savior, Jesus Christ.

Satan has an eight-point plan to destroy the church. We need to be aware of the points taught by Satan to his servants to use in destroying a Christian church:

1. The Satanist must be converted.

The Satanist must become "converted." In order to gain credibility with the members of the local church and the pastor, the Satanist pretends to be saved. Usually, the person will come to the altar or the prayer room and have a "dynamic conversion." He or she will do whatever is expected to give a sign of this "conversion." Then, after the profession of faith is established, he or she will begin to rapidly gain wonderful spiritual insights and "grow" by leaps and bounds to the point where they often pass long-established Christians or even the pastor in spiritual wisdom and insights.

If the person doesn't go to the altar for his conversion, then he'll show up at the church as a "supersaint" with all kinds of spiritual insights and truths but with a very hazy history of when, where, or how he became a Christian. Again, his or her wisdom will soon surpass that of those who are already established in the church.

Charismatic churches are especially vulnerable because the new "supersaint" will manifest all of the "gifts" to establish his superior credibility. Satan can counterfeit all of the "gifts of the Spirit," but there is one thing Satan can't do. Satan cannot *love*. We need to test the spirits in each situation and not just accept a person at face value. We're directed in scripture to test the spirits:

> Beloved, believe not every spirit, but try the spirits whether they are of God: because many false prophets are gone out into the world. Hereby know ye the Spirit of God: Every spirit that confesseth that Jesus Christ is come in the flesh is of God: And every spirit that confesseth not that Jesus Christ is come in the flesh is not of God: and this is that spirit of antichrist, whereof ye have heard that it should come; and even now already is it in the world. (1 John 4:1-3)

And he said, Take heed that ye be not deceived: for many shall come in my name. (Luke 21:8)

> Not every one that saith unto me, Lord, Lord, shall enter into the kingdom of heaven; but he that doeth the will of my Father which is in heaven. Many will say to me in that day, Lord, Lord, have we not prophesied in thy name and in thy name have cast out devils? and in thy name done many wonderful works? And then will I profess unto them, I never knew you: depart from me, ye that work iniquity. (Matt. 7:21-28)

Too many Christians are confused about how Satan works. Satanists *can* and *do* use the name of Jesus. They can teach and preach about Jesus. They can even use the name of Jesus when they pray. I had one fellow in my church who prayed quoting scripture back to God because "he was praying God's own Word and promises." But according to 1 John 4, they can't look you in the face and say, "Jesus Christ who is God, who came in the flesh, died on the cross and three days later arose from the dead and now sits at the right hand of God the Father, this Jesus is my Lord and Savior and Master." They can confess "Jesus saved me," but you don't really know, which Jesus they are confessing. Jesus took time to warn us that many would come claiming to be Him. Satan doesn't care what lies he tells. He is the father of all liars according to Jesus. A Satanist can lie and say yes if you ask him if he serves Jesus Christ who came in the flesh, but he can't bring himself to the confession out of his own mouth as given above.

2. The Satanist will build credibility.

There are many ways for Satanists to build credibility for themselves within the Christian churches, depending on the worship style of the particular church. They attend the services regularly. They are always ready and willing to help in any project. They get to know the church members and the pastor. They soon find out who is really committed to Jesus Christ and who is not.

Money is an important tool in building credibility. In the large churches with enough wealth, they give regularly, gradually increasing the amounts they give until they have become one of the main supporters in the church financially. It's surprising how much influence money can buy in the running of a church!

In small churches where money is a premium, the people usually seem quite poor. The Satanist doesn't flash around a lot of money but gradually and carefully increase their giving until many of the programs are dependent upon their financial support. This way they lead the church the direction they want to go because the leaders of the church are afraid of losing the financial support.

I've had the opportunity of seeing this method of church control work by firsthand experience. I've never felt that God needs people's money to run His program, so I've never "bowed and scraped" to moneyed people. However, some of my church-board members have been influenced from time to time by fat bank accounts and have been willing to compromise and accommodate convictions to keep the money flowing. Let me say God isn't dependent upon man's money. God can find resources without compromising our convictions to do the work that God wants done. God isn't for sale. We can't be either! We should never let anyone's money buy power and prestige in the church!

3. The Satanist will try to destroy the prayer base.

The primary goal of any Satanist is to stop people from praying. Satan doesn't want you to pray! Prayer moves the hand of God in our lives. When we don't pray, we don't communicate with God, and we tie God's hands in helping us. The nonpraying church is a weak, anemic church that isn't doing much for the kingdom of God. That's the kind of church Satan loves because he doesn't have to worry about that church.

Usually, the prayer base is destroyed in a very subtle manner with full cooperation of the church leadership because they think what they're doing will benefit the church. My church in Arizona had an active prayer ministry going, and the church was growing by leaps and bounds.

A couple from the area came into our congregation and began to establish themselves in positions of leadership. They seemed burdened over the number of poor and hungry people in the community. They began to promote the idea that the church should pray for these people and provide food for the needy. They even helped finance food for a big dinner to "reach" souls in the neighborhood. The congregation was excited!

Interestingly enough, the couple came to see how many people had shown up for the dinner, but they refused to come into the fellowship hall where it was being served because "they were too bashful and self-conscious to be around so many folks that they didn't know."

The next step was to recommend to our congregation that we spend less time praying about these poor folks and more time ministering and calling upon them. "God has heard our prayers and now it's time to put feet to our prayers and reach out to these people."

From there, they suggested the Wednesday evening prayer service could be better used by having small cell groups who would spend a little time in prayer and a lot of time in outreach. The plan sounded good to an unsuspecting congregation because we do need to go out into the "highways and byways and compel them to come in" to hear the Gospel!

This is usually the method used in one form or another. It might be that we need Wednesday for choir practice because our schedules are so busy that we've no other time to practice and prepare for a wonderful worship service on Sunday, or Wednesday prayer time could be better invested in strong youth program because our kids face so many problems today and really need to know they have our support, or any one of a hundred other plans to neutralize the prayer base. Usually, the plan to spend less time in prayer makes sense because it will give us time to minister more effectively.

Once the prayer base is neutralized, so is the growth of the church. In fact, the church soon begins to go downhill because of problems and misunderstandings. It isn't long until the church is either helpless or hopeless.

4. There are lots of rumors!

Once the prayer base of the church has been destroyed, the Satanists are free to do whatever they want to do. One of the basic tools is rumors. Gossip is Satan's favorite tool. Not many people are strong enough to keep from passing on an interesting tidbit that they have heard. Rumors can easily destroy the credibility of the pastor and the real Christians in a church.

Many times in the last forty-four years of ministry, I've had to come up against this ploy, which Satan and his people use so well. Gossip gets started and runs like wildfire in a dry forest being whipped by the wind. Without a prayer base, it seems there's no way to stop such gossip until it has run its destructive course.

Church leaders need to be careful at all times. *Never* go alone to the home of a member or friend of the church if the person is of the opposite sex. This is especially true if you plan to help or counsel them. (I've dealt with this problem in the chapter, Lest Ye Fall.) It's so easy to have lies told about the incident even if you did nothing to compromise your convictions. Who can prove it if charges are made? Too many pastors' careers have been destroyed by just such mistakes. First Thessalonians 5:22 says, "Abstain from all appearance of evil." How we need to pay attention!

5. Satanists want to teach and change vital doctrines.

A Satanist wants to get into a teaching position in the church. He can do tremendous damage in such a position. Are you really aware of where all of your Sunday school teachers stand with the Lord? Have you monitored what they're teaching to your children?

When I was a boy in a preteen Sunday school class in the First Church of the Nazarene in Walla Walla, Washington, I had a Sunday school teacher that was trying to teach my class how to "speak in tongues." She'd spend whole sessions telling us about "tongues" and how to "pick a phrase" so we could get started in this very special experience that the Church of the Nazarene didn't practice or encourage. Finally, I asked my pastor what she was trying to teach us. He came "uncorked!" The next Sunday we had a new teacher. Now the point isn't to argue for or against the speaking in tongues, but the point is that this woman was offering to a class of fifth and sixth graders training that wasn't endorsed by the church. Can you see how much damage this could cause? Something like this can be very divisive in a church. There are many teachers in churches who aren't trying to build the church and God's kingdom, but who are trying to destroy God's work. What a shame to think of time wasted by not teaching the students the true Gospel of Jesus Christ! I had another "teacher" when I was in high school who spent his time teaching his very liberal concepts that were in no way related to the stands and doctrines of the church. He did much damage to some of the young people. Several have left the church and the Lord and will probably lose their souls for eternity in hell.

It's not only some teachers who have infiltrated the ranks of the church. There are Satanists in many pulpits today. Some of these pulpits are in large and wealthy churches that have far-reaching influence. The people in the congregations are too lazy to study their Bibles to check out what they're hearing and being taught and are being led down paths of destruction. There are several basic areas Satanists teach most about:

a. Prayer. Prayer is presented as very complex and complicated. It's often taught that there are many steps believers must go through before they can even begin to be in a "right" relationship with God and have any power in prayer. God won't even hear them if they've not followed this exact formula. They twist scriptures and lift verses out of context to teach their false concepts. It becomes so confusing that many people just give up trying to pray at all. That is what Satan wants because he doesn't want people to pray! It would be well to check what Hebrews 4:14-16 has to say:

> Seeing then that we have a great high priest, that is passed into the heavens, Jesus the Son of God, let us hold fast our profession. For we have not an high priest which cannot be touched with the feeling of our infirmities; but was in all points tempted like as we are, yet without sin. Let us therefore come boldly unto the throne of grace, that we may obtain mercy, and find grace to help in time of need. (Heb. 4:14-16)

b. Probably the most dangerous and destructive thing being taught today by Satanists is the health-and-wealth message. The idea is that "God wants all of His children to be healthy and wealthy." If someone is suffering in their physical being or is experiencing financial problems or is being persecuted in any way, it's because they don't have a right relationship with Christ, or they don't have faith to receive what Christ wants them to have. I've known genuine Christians who went through hellish torment because they were sick and didn't have enough faith to claim wholeness. My own mother just about lost her faith over this very issue before her death in 1986. She had been told over and over that if she was in a right standing with Christ, she wouldn't be sick. There had to be something wrong with her relationship with God. She was obviously just too sinful; otherwise, God would have healed her!

These are lies right out of hell designed to torment Christians when they're very vulnerable anyway. The scriptures that show how false this doctrine is are numerous. One of the strongest verses that cover this matter is 2 Timothy 3:12,

> Yea, and all that will live godly in Christ Jesus shall suffer persecution. (2 Tim. 3:12)

Note that it doesn't say what kind of persecutions the believer will suffer—it could be financial, physical, or emotional.

c. Another lie that goes hand-in-hand or maybe is part of the health-and-wealth teaching is the "name-it-claim-it" doctrine. If you've enough faith, you can speak whatever you want, and God has to give it to you! If you want more money or a bigger house or a nicer car or just about anything, just speak it in faith, and it's yours! Wow! Talk about a doctrine that's based on selfishness! What do you suppose ever happened to the concept that Jesus taught in the Gospels, "If any man will come after me, let him deny himself, take up his cross, and follow me" (Matt. 16:24)?

d. The "seed-faith" teachings also fall into an area of selfish false doctrine. If you want a greater income, just tithe on the income that you want to have. God will then be obligated to provide the wealth that you've claimed. This is especially true if you will send that tithe amount in to one of the ministers that is espousing this "truth." My observation has been that the minister gets rich and can testify how this works while the poor, deluded person who has acted on this concept usually is out the amount that they've selfishly set in to ensure increased income but never seem to get the added wealth.

e. Finally, Satan has developed the "love doctrine"—"we can't judge anybody." Satanists protect themselves with this doctrine, and passive Christians are careful not to step on anyone's toes.

Knowing someone "by their fruits" and judging someone are two different matters! Jesus said, "Beware of false prophets, which come to you in sheep's clothing, but inwardly they are ravening wolves. Ye shall know them by their fruits" (Matt. 7:15-16).

You can't judge, but you can be "fruit inspectors." As Christians, we don't have to be stupid! We can have enough sense to know when something isn't right!

One of the greatest tactics used when Satan's trying to destroy a church is to convince everybody that there is "no spiritual food" in the sermons. For years, I've been accused of "giving no spiritual food." Usually, it's an accusation that comes from somebody who is under conviction and doesn't want to admit that God is trying to bring them to Himself. It's easier to blame the pastor for feeling miserable than it is to swallow pride and get things straightened out with God.

6. Satanists try to break up family units.

Divide and conquer! Satan knows that if he can successfully break up the family unit, he will also break apart the unity of the church. Satanists that have infiltrated Christian churches work hard to separate families. They want to start all kinds of programs for teens, for children, and for preschoolers. They also try to create separate programs for men and women, to keep the parents separated as much as possible.

Children need to hear sermons and join in to worship services and prayer meetings as much as the adults do! When are children going to learn how to worship and respond to God if they are kept isolated and entertained? The Bible teaches the principle that children learn through the training and example of the parents. The children learn by joining in with parents. Children learn respect both for God and the church by learning to sit in the worship service and listen to the pastor. When programs are developed for young people separating them from the mainstream church, they begin to lose respect for the church and the pastor. They no longer have to stay and listen to the sermon—it's just too boring! It's not long until there is little or no interest in spiritual things. Children just want to come to church to be entertained. If they no longer feel entertained, they're no longer interested in coming to church and usually drop out in their early teen years.

There is no better way for children to learn to pray and worship than by participating in the services with their parents. The home is constantly under attack by Satan. It's important that the home is centered upon Christ.

The family needs to stay unified. Separating them within the church is a giant step toward driving wedges between the family members.

7. Satanists want you to stop all accurate teaching about Satan!

The pastor told me, "I believe that if we leave Satan alone that he will leave us alone!"

I'd just finished a seminar on spiritual warfare, and he had taken exception to what I was teaching. Of course Satan wants us to ignore him and leave him alone. That way he can do his work without being detected. I promise you this: Just because you leave him alone doesn't mean that he is going to leave you alone. He's just counting on the fact that you might be dumb enough to think that! The fact is he hopes you are that dumb! Listen to what the scriptures teach us:

> Lest Satan should get an advantage of us: for we are not ignorant of his devices. (2 Cor. 2:11)

> My people are destroyed for lack of knowledge: because thou hast rejected knowledge, I will also reject thee, that thou shalt be no priest to me: seeing thou hast forgotten the law of thy God, I will also forget thy children. (Hosea 4:6)

> Be sober, be vigilant; because your adversary the devil, as a roaring lion, walketh about seeking whom he may devour. (1 Pet. 5:8)

> And this is the condemnation, that light is come into the world, and men loved darkness rather than light, because their deeds were evil. (John 3:19)

One of Satan's main objectives is to stop any teaching about him and what he is doing.

If he can keep people ignorant about what he is doing, he'll be relatively unhindered in anything he decides to do. Satanists are always instructed to stop any teaching about the devil in the churches they attend.

They usually use the same basic arguments as to why the church shouldn't teach about Satan. "Teaching about Satan gives glory to him." "It takes people's minds off God." "It tempts people to turn to Satan." And it goes on and on.

God's Word clearly teaches about Satan. It warns us that if we remain ignorant about our adversary that he will destroy us. It's time for Christians to wake up and realize what the stakes that are in this war that we should be waging. If I don't believe that Satan is busy in my home and my church, then I won't be working against him to win souls for Jesus. I learned a poem years ago that every Christian needs to memorize:

> Six days a week the devil works
> And overtime on Sunday.
> Then he's ready once again
> To go to work on Monday.
> Now if evil you would shun
> And keep you conscience level,
> You must get up early every day
> And work just like the devil!
>
> —Author unknown

8. Satanists use direct attacks by witchcraft against pastor and church.

Someone is going to say, "Come on! How far out can you get? This is America, and we are living in modern times!" That's precisely the problem! America has turned back to paganism! For years, our missionaries have fought witchcraft on foreign fields. Now we have to fight the same forces here. I'm dealing more and more with pastors, key laymen, and churches that are under severe attack by witches and demonic forces. In fact, I have dealt firsthand with these kinds of attacks. I will give illustrations in other parts of this book.

The fact that we are being bombarded with witchcraft is another reason why prayer is so important. Any pastors or church members that are really taking a stand for Jesus Christ and against the devil will be subject to tremendous attack by witchcraft.

We can expect all kinds of physical illness, difficulties in concentrating, confusion, fatigue, difficulties in praying, etc. The people must learn to hold their spiritual leaders up in prayer and intercede for them. When that prayer base is lost, the pastor and the leaders will have to face these attacks alone. Too often that's when they're overcome and suffer defeat. The apostle Paul was continually asking for his Christian supporters to pray for him that he be not defeated.

Satan has had a heyday in America! The powerless, anemic churches across our land being led by ignorant, wishy-washy pastors who are afraid to preach the truth is a testimony of how Satan has succeeded in his program. Pray that our pastors and churches will wake up and learn how to fight the attacks of Satan on the church today!

THE IMPOSTOR

It was Friday afternoon, and I was busy with the Fishing Hole, the youth center that our church provided for the neighborhood children and teens. Somebody told me there was a phone call for me in the kitchen, and it was long distance. I hurried to the phone hoping that it wasn't anything too major that would require a lot of time and effort. I was tired!

The voice on the line identified himself as Richard Knight. He said he was in trouble and had heard that I could provide a place of safety and help. He further informed me that he had helped a girl in New York City escape from a coven of witches. Now the angry coven members were trying to kill him. He was afraid that they would succeed.

"Where are you now?" I asked.

"In Boston," he replied, "I'm hiding, and I think that I am safe for the moment, but I really need to get out of here as quickly as I can!"

I said, "I can have a place ready for you by Monday. Can you hold out that long?"

His answer indicated that he thought he would be safe until Monday. We made plans for me to meet him at the Phoenix International Airport next Monday evening—just three short days away!

On Monday evening, I was at the air terminal at the appointed time. The flight would be about ten minutes late, but everything else seemed to be OK.

I was surprised when nobody fitting the description that Richard had given me got off the plane. I asked the airline desk if he'd been on that flight. They had no record of a *Richard Knight* on that particular flight.

I asked the operator on the "white paging phone" to have Richard Knight paged. Still no response!

Finally, desperate but not knowing what to do, I gave up and went home confused and concerned about what might've happened to Richard.

Sometime after 11:00 p.m., the phone rang. The voice on the other end of the line said that it was Richard Knight. He told me that he'd gotten caught in traffic in Boston and had missed his original flight. He now was in Phoenix. Would I come get him?

The voice seemed different, but I assumed that he was tired. Besides, I'd only spoken to him once before and on a different telephone, and there had been confusion in the room when we had spoken. Maybe I was just paranoid.

The fellow that was waiting for me at the airport was strange! His manners were crude. He snorted and coughed and fidgeted. His gestures were abrupt and jerky. His conversation seemed strained, and he wasn't open with any information about himself, which I felt I needed. After all, I was risking my life and my family to help him.

I didn't like this guy! I would be happy to send him on his way as quickly as possible. "Maybe it will be better tomorrow." I told myself. But by the next day things hadn't improved.

By the following Friday, I knew that I had a real problem. Who was this person that had invaded my domain anyway?

To make matters worse, I received a phone call from a young lady who used to be a witch but now was serving Jesus Christ. She told me that she had heard about this person that was now in my care. She began to describe him to me. His appearance, his mannerisms, his personality, on and on she went. "How do you know all this?" I asked. She told me she had once worked with this man to infiltrate another Christian ministry. She said he was no good, that he was dangerous, and that I'd better get him away from my church and people as quickly as possible. His name wasn't Richard Knight but was Bruce Kenny, and he was high up in occult circles. He was a known assassin for the Satanists!

Naturally, this kind of information "thrilled my heart!" What was I going to do now? *Dear God!* I said, *Why did you let something like this happen to me? I just want to help people. I don't want this kind of thing!*

I decided upon a plan of action. I'd take this individual, whoever he was, with me to pick up the supplies for the Fishing Hole. I asked my wife and two other people from our congregation to go into the house this fellow was using and see what they could find.

The news wasn't good! They'd found a voodoo altar in his room with all kinds of strange objects on and around it. He had apparently been trying to put some kind of a curse on my church people and on me. There were many other things throughout the house that were demonic in nature. This man certainly wasn't who he'd said that he was. What had happened to the real Richard Knight?

I had dropped this impostor off at the house where he was staying before I went to my office to receive this troubling report. Now I had to go back to the house, enter, and confront this agent of Satan. I had to get him off the property before he caused more havoc. One of my church board members went with me for the confrontation. We had prayer and put on our spiritual armor for protection (refer to the chapter on spiritual armor). Even then, it took all the courage that I could muster to go and knock on that door.

The strange man answered the door, and I pushed my way passed him and inside the house. He seemed surprised that I could enter the door so easily. He had smeared a mixture of blood and oil on the door jam and had posted demons there to keep out unwanted folks. Obviously, he'd thought his plan would work. He was totally surprised because his demon at the door had no power against the true servants of God. Both my board member and I entered the house in the power of Jesus Christ!

I asked him what his name really was because I knew that he was an impostor. He said that his name really was Richard Knight.

I told him that I knew he was lying through his teeth, and I wasn't going to put up with it any longer.

He said, "All right, my name isn't Richard Knight. I was told by the people who told me about you to use that name because it would be safer if I didn't use my real name."

"You're still lying!" I said. "Your name is Bruce Kenny, and you're an infiltrator for a satanic organization bent on doing damage to God's kingdom!"

He said, "I'm not a Satanist! I'm a believer."

"Then, who is your master?" I responded. "Who do you serve?"

He replied, "I serve God, the creator of the universe."

I answered, "That won't wash! Now tell me who you really serve!"

He stuttered and stammered but never could confess that Jesus is the Son of God who came to earth in the flesh. According to 1 John 4:15, anyone who serves God ought to be able to make this confession.

I told him to pack his things because I wanted him off of the property that very afternoon.

I should've stayed right with him until he was ready to go back to the airport, but I had to run the early session of the Fishing Hole. It was Friday afternoon, and a couple hundred kids from the neighborhood would soon be there.

Finally, around 5:00 p.m., I took him to a departure flight away from Phoenix. He had two hours to get his things together before I took him to his plane. During that time, he put all kinds of curses and hexes on the house and property.

When I went back to the house, I noticed something was very strange and unusual. The sheets on the bed where he'd slept had been white with tan stripes when he arrived. Now they were white with purple stripes! Other things were amiss also.

I called Betsy (not her real name), a once powerful witch, but who was now a Christian. She had lived in Las Vegas and was known for her position in the craft. Betsy told me what to look for in the house: strange coins, bent nails, oil and/or blood smears, objects that seemed strange or out of place, keys, doorknobs, hinges, pins, marbles, crystals, pieces of mirrors, and things like that. She warned that I should wear rubber gloves when handling these items. They could be very dangerous to handle without proper protection. She instructed me to check in corners, under rugs, behind vents, in drains, in windows, under beds, in furniture—everywhere!

She said to burn the sheets because they had a curse upon them, and the next person to sleep on them could be open to a lot of demonic trouble. "It could be especially bad," she said, "if they have any kind of sexual relationship upon those sheets."

The board member and I went to work! We found about half a mixing bowl full of items Betsy had described. We burned the sheets and, to my surprise, they melted down like Styrofoam leaving little or no residue behind.

We anointed the house with oil (check the chapter on Anointing with Oil). We rebuked and bound and expelled all demons in the name of Jesus Christ.

I should mention that I found several pentagrams on the walls of the house, and we had to anoint and pray over each one in the name of Jesus Christ.

I thought this chapter was over, and the strange person was only history as far as I was concerned. *Dream on, Preacher!* Satan doesn't take kindly to having his plans foiled. He is the "destroyer," and he'll do all he can to bring death and destruction to any who oppose him. *Thank God, Satan can do no more than God will permit him to do!*

About a week after I'd sent this impostor away, I received a phone call from some of my friends in Los Angeles, California. They said the real Richard Knight had been caught by the Satanist coven and had been sacrificed. He had died victoriously, and some of the witches and warlocks who witnessed his murder had later renounced Satan and turned to Jesus Christ. Praise the Lord! Satan can't keep God from final victory no matter how hard he tries or how much evil he inspires!

That was the good news, but there was some other news to share too. It didn't sound so great! In fact, it was horrible news as far as I was concerned! The caller said that her group had been praying, and God had revealed to them that Satan had petitioned for my little granddaughter's life in retribution for what I'd done to Bruce Kenny. The baby was supposed to die at 1:00 p.m., Friday, if God granted this petition. That was the next afternoon! It was now 11:55 p.m. on Thursday night! My wife and I felt panic surge through us! Certainly God wouldn't allow this to happen! Would He?

We immediately went to prayer. Satan had asked for my grandbaby's life, but Satan is an enemy of God. *I'm an adopted son of God, one of his own—purchased with the precious blood of Jesus Christ!* Certainly, God will listen to His own child before He listens to the requests of His enemy!

I remembered Jesus had said, "If you then, being evil, know how to give good gifts unto your children, how much more shall your Father which is in Heaven give good things to them that ask Him" (Matt. 7:11, KJV)?

My wife and I had a season of prayer that night pleading with God for help and mercy in behalf of our beautiful little granddaughter. We counterpetitioned Satan's request and knew that God had heard our prayers.

The next morning I was at my daughter's home at 7:00 a.m. I woke her up! I asked her if I could pray with the baby and anoint her and the house with oil.

She said, "Daddy, what's wrong?"

I tried to assure her that nothing was wrong, that I just wanted to pray a blessing on her little girl.

She saw it was more than that and kept pressing the issue until finally, I told her about the late call last night and what was taking place. She was immediately enveloped in panic and hysteria.

I told her, "Stop that and get a hold on yourself! God has revealed this to us so that we and He can do something about it! Your baby will be OK, but we don't have time to panic now!"

She managed to regain her composure.

I prayed for our precious baby. I then anointed the house and rebuked, bound, and expelled demons in the name of Jesus Christ. There was a calm in the house now.

It was decided our daughter and granddaughter should come to our parsonage and spend the day near my wife since our son-in-law was at work, and our daughter was anxious about being alone that day.

All of us spent much time in prayer and soul-searching that day!

Around noon, the baby was asleep in the guest bedroom. My youngest daughter, the baby's aunt, slipped in to check upon the baby to see if she was all right. She suddenly called to my wife, "MOM! COME IN HERE NOW!"

Sensing urgency, my wife dropped everything she was doing and ran to the bedroom.

The baby was still asleep, but one of her legs had turned black, and the black was moving up in to her torso. My wife grabbed the anointing oil and anointed the sleeping baby in the name of the Father, Son, and Holy Spirit. She rebuked the devil and his demons. She broke every hex and incantation in the name of Jesus.

Soon the color started to come back in to the baby's leg and body. She slept on.

Finally, at 2:00 p.m., one hour after she was supposed to die according to Satan's scheme, she woke up just as happy and bubbly as any baby that you've ever seen. *Praise God! The crisis is over!* His children had the victory!

Later, I asked God in prayer, *Why did we have to go through that ordeal? It was frightening!*

His answer, *Because I want you to realize what you're doing is very real and that you can depend on my Power for protection as you do My will.*

I don't know what happened to the impostor, Bruce Kenny. I do know that he's serving a loser by sticking with Satan!

But as for me and my household, we will serve the LORD!
(Josh. 24:15)

HOW SATAN TORMENTS US

She called the parsonage just before midnight and was beside herself with panic. "I've destroyed the church with my big mouth!" she wailed. "I didn't mean to say the things that I said! It is all my fault! I am so wicked! I don't think God can forgive me this time!"

It was Velma (not her real name), one of the faithful old "pillars" of the church. I couldn't imagine what she was talking about. Velma is one of the sweetest most thoughtful older ladies in my congregation. I knew that whatever had happened, Satan was blowing it all out of proportion this late night. He knew she lived alone and hadn't been feeling well. It was late at night (one of his favorite times to attack), and he had been busy tormenting this poor soul about a comment she'd made to my wife concerning one of the children in our church. She had been upset at how the little girl had acted during a worship service. Now Satan was telling Velma that her comment was going to spread through the church. The little girl's family would get upset and leave the church. Many of their friends and loved ones would join them in a great exodus away from the church. The little girl would become bitter and eventually lose her soul and on and on. All this would occur because of a passing comment spoken in the heat of frustration.

It was time for the invitation at the end of the evangelistic worship service. The altar was opened, and seekers were invited to come pray. Lynn (not his real name) broke from his place in the sanctuary and literally bolted down the aisle and fell across the altar sobbing his heart out to God for mercy. Soon his wife came and knelt beside him saying, "Lynn, I thought that I would come and help you pray." I knelt on the other side of the altar rail and asked Lynn what we were praying about.

He said he didn't know what the problem was, but he had this awful feeling that something was not right—that he was failing as a Christian, a husband, and a dad. He couldn't think of any deliberate sin he'd committed, but something was making him miserable.

Bill was a devout Christian teenager. He'd accepted Jesus as his savior when he was quite young. He had read his Bible, prayed, tried to obey God at every opportunity. He felt a "call from God" to dedicate his life to being a missionary. He wanted to go to New Guinea or Africa or some other dark country to proclaim the good news of Christ's love and salvation for men and women. Bill's home wasn't a Christian home. In fact, Bill's dad was doing everything he could to destroy his son's faith so Bill wouldn't throw his life away serving God "like some old lady!" There was also pressure on Bill from his peers because of his weight problem and because of his Christian walk, which wouldn't permit him to indulge in some of the things that others his age were doing. His peers thought he was some kind of a killjoy, and they ostracized him from their activities.

Bill thanked God for godly grandparents who often were the stabilizing factor for his Christian walk. Suddenly, for no apparent reason, Bill was placed under demonic attack and was almost destroyed. A blasphemous thought would come into his mind and immediately the accuser would begin to taunt, "Christians don't think like that! You have committed the 'unpardonable sin!' You're going to end up in hell, and there is nothing you can do about it because God no longer loves you after you had that thought!" Bill was ashamed over what was happening! He couldn't turn to his dad for help. He was afraid to talk to his pastor because he didn't want the pastor to know what thoughts were running in his mind. The only person he could turn to was his grandmother. Each night, he would call in a desperate panic saying, "Grandma, do you think I'm OK? I've tried to pray, and I just can't seem to get through. I'm so worried that if I died I would go to hell."

She would say, "Bill, have you done any sin that you can think of today?" He would say, "No, I have tried to live for Jesus all day long." She would then say, "Billy, I think you're all right. Just pray and ask God to show you if you have done anything wrong. If you don't remember something that you have done in rebellion to God, then quote Psalms 4:8 and go to sleep. God loves you and will protect you!" Psalms 4:8 says, "I will both lay me down in peace, and sleep: for thou, LORD, only makest me to dwell in safety."

To the casual observer it might seem that Velma, Lynn, and Bill have all "slipped a cog" or "the driveway does not go all the way to the top." I assure you that this isn't the case. Each of these individuals are normal and aren't bent toward "weird." Each was under spiritual attack from Satan and his demonic forces. Every true Christian is a potential target for just such an attack. Because of this, I feel that saints need to learn to identify the difference between old-time conviction from God and satanic torment of a tender spirit trying to please God.

It's an obvious understatement to say that Satan is cruel and doesn't fight fairly. First Peter 5:8 says that Satan walks around as a "roaring lion seeking whom he may devour." The lion usually has better success in capturing the young and the weak. The same seems to be true with the devil. When we understand how he works, we'll not be so vulnerable to his onslaught of attacks.

The first thing that needs to be understood is that "Satan is the accuser of the brethren." He accuses us before the throne of God. He accuses us before other Christians. He often accuses us to our own selves. He tells us something is dreadfully wrong with our relationship with God. He tells us we've failed so badly that God isn't even interested in us anymore. He tells us that we're lost and hopeless! I've dealt with scores, perhaps hundreds, of Christians during the last forty-four years who've suffered agony over these unfounded and unfair accusations. You must remember that what Satan says isn't based on fact. He is a liar and the father of all liars (John 8:44)! He'll tell you anything that he thinks will bring torment to you.

When Satan attacks us, he just says something is wrong, but he never is specific as to what it might be. When God deals with us about sin, He is always specific and clear about where the problem lies. We're never in doubt as to what He's showing us. Satan never gives us a plan to change the situation. God always shows us what we must do to bridge the broken relationship.

Lynn came to the altar, not because God was convicting him of sin, but because Satan was harassing him with false guilt and condemnation. Now that Lynn understands what is going on, he'll be able to contend with Satan's false accusations and guilt. He can walk in a right relationship with God through faith and not just feeling. God honors His word. When we have confessed our sins and He has forgiven our sins and cleansed us from all unrighteousness (1 John 1:9), He doesn't bring our sins up again. They're covered by His blood and forgotten by God. Psalm 103:12 says, "As far as the east is from the west, so far hath He removed our transgressions from us." God never torments us about sin just to see us squirm. Any sin that He brings to our mind is real, and we understand what He is pointing out to us.

Another technique the devil uses is to put a thought in our mind and make us think that we thought of it ourselves. He usually does this by starting the thought with "I" or "my." Because we're used to that we seldom question where the thought is coming from and how it lodged into our mind. After the thought has occurred, he begins to make accusations that Christians don't think like that, and if we really had a right relationship with God, we wouldn't be thinking like that either. Something must be terribly wrong with a spiritual walk that allows such evil to even be thought in the first place. This thought pattern goes on until the poor victim begins to doubt his salvation.

That's exactly the dilemma that Satan had Bill going through at the beginning of this chapter. Satan would plant blasphemous thoughts in Bill's mind and then stand back and accuse him of cursing the Holy Spirit or entertaining filthy thoughts. Bill would panic and try to pray about his relationship to God, but the demonic forces would put up such a barrage that Bill couldn't find peace. Naturally, he felt that God was not answering him when, in reality, God was right there, but Satan had him worked to such a fever pitch that Bill couldn't hear God. Bill had worked himself in to that old pattern, "when in trouble or in doubt, run in circles, scream, and shout." Thank God that Bill had a concerned grandmother who could pray for him, encourage him, and calm him.

Someone will usually ask, "can Satan or his demons read our mind." No! Satan is not omniscient. Only God can read minds and thoughts. Satanic forces do study the individual and pick up on how he reacts to certain stimuli. He can make an educated guess on what is going on in the thought processes and act accordingly. More will be said about this topic in the chapter on familiar spirits.

Among the devil's greatest ploys is the one where he convinces a person that some sin has been committed that has disqualified the person for heaven. Just as a word of encouragement, let me assure you that Satan can't put something so deep in the human heart, but that the blood of Jesus Christ can go even deeper. There's not one sin that can be committed if the Holy Spirit is bringing conviction and the person really wants to repent, which cannot be forgiven by Jesus Christ! You're not too evil or sinful to come to Christ for cleansing! You're not hopeless if you want hope! The key is genuine repentance and a changing of life's direction. "If you confess your sins He is faithful and just to forgive your sins and to cleanse you from all unrighteousness" (1 John 1:9). Praise God!

Satan often causes misunderstandings between Christians and stirs up trouble in their lives and in the church. The situation with Velma described above was just such an example. The little girl that caused Velma the frustration would sit in front of Velma during the worship service and make all sorts of ugly little faces. I believe the child was probably bored and was just seeking some form of quiet entertainment to occupy her time until the service was finished. Satan began to put thoughts into Velma's mind that this child was doing this to show her contempt and dislike for Velma. Soon the thoughts were coming that "this child was probably reflecting an attitude that she had heard in her home. Probably her parents and grandparents had singled Velma out and were saying mean and cruel things about her during the week in their home. In fact, they were probably gossiping about Velma around the dinner table on a regular basis." The more Velma thought about this, the more destructive thoughts and suspicions the demons fed into Velma's mind. It wasn't long until everything was blown way out of proportion, and the only solution that Velma could think of was to leave the church. Satan was rejoicing over this major victory! Thank God, it was pointed out to Velma what was happening, and she prayed to God for forgiveness about her attitude and put the whole matter in God's care. She is back attending church again and able to concentrate on her worship of God. Imagine how defeating it would have been to everyone involved if Velma had just stopped going to church!

What happened to Velma with one of the children in the church often happens to adult Christians too. Satan will cause some miscommunication between church members (usually something minor), and then he'll proceed to make it a bigger and bigger problem in the church until things are blown out of proportion, and people are taking sides against one another. Be warned; demons twist words and thoughts in communication, and if the people involved aren't careful to straighten things out, Christ's kingdom can be damaged. I'll illustrate—the piano player at our church overslept and had another man phone the church saying that he'd be late for the worship service. I told the individual that had placed the call to tell the pianist that when he came into the sanctuary to please wait before approaching the piano bench until he was told to come up so he didn't disturb the flow of the service. I didn't know what God might be doing in the service at that time. The man that I told this information to went to the pianist and said, "Since you are late, the pastor doesn't want you to play the piano today!" This hurt the pianist's feelings. If I hadn't caught what was happening and headed off the misunderstanding, this could've turned into a very difficult problem in our church.

Another recent illustration might shed even more light to the point I want to drive home. It had been a wonderful morning service! There were ten seekers at the altar, and all of them seemed to get help. I went home rejoicing because of what God was doing in our church. We had prayed for revival. Was this the beginning of what had been the longing of our hearts for so long? God had certainly shown Himself in that service! The preaching had been inspired. It was one of those times when God had anointed every word that had been spoken.

I was still basking in the warmth of that wonderful service when I arrived back to the church to have our worship-team practice before the evening service. Things seemed to go well for the practice. I saw I had time to run next door (our parsonage was next door to the church building) and care for a few last-second matters before the evening service began. I was only gone for five minutes. When I returned to the sanctuary, things were in shambles! The piano player and the guitar player had had a dispute over recording a special musical number, which we'd scheduled for the service. One of the older ladies in the congregation had heard them disputing and said, "Attitude! Attitude!" This set the guitarist off in a carnal rage, and he stomped out of the room. His daughter spoke sharply and with disrespect to the lady reminding her that she was just an "old lady," and this was really none of her business. The pianist's stepdaughter heard what the other girl was saying and began to air her views on what was going on and what the other girl had said. By the time I got back to the pulpit, half the congregation had gotten involved in this dispute, and most of them were in a rage.

I didn't know what had transpired until after the service. I didn't understand why we couldn't get the service off of the ground and why the sermon seemed so flat and hard to preach after the glorious service that morning. It was a good sermon! It should've done better than it did!

After the evening service, the pianist resigned. The guitarist wasn't going to play in the service again. The lady who had been accused of being old and nosy was saying, "Well, I am old," and one man who hadn't even been there that evening, who had heard about what had occurred, called me and said that he would probably not come back to church if that was the way Christians treated each other. He said he thought the guitarist was too pompous and stuck-up and so was his family. He accused the guitarist of thinking that he was the pastor and was running things around the church.

I guess the man felt badly for missing the main scrimmage and wanted to get into the fight as much as he possibly could at this late hour. It must be frustrating to want to be in a good church fight and miss the one night that one takes place! It shows that you shouldn't miss the evening service!

I went home reeling over all that had transpired. Was this really the same congregation who had celebrated such a wonderful morning blessing? Where were we going to go from here? How could I be the peacemaker to make all the wrongs right? Certainly, what had happened wasn't of God—it was a demonic attack!

Later, another lady in the church called me and demanded that the teenage girl apologize to the "old lady" (the caller's mother) for her rudeness and bad attitude. Will this thing never end?

The truth is that what had happened *was* demonically inspired. Satan wasn't pleased about the victories during the morning service. He wanted to rob any blessing the people felt as a result of that spiritual outpouring from God. It looked like the demons knew their business! The entire evening service was a wipeout! Satan's forces must've felt that they had scored a major victory!

How we need to keep in tune with Jesus and be certain that we don't let the devil play games in our minds and use us for his purposes! It seems that demons can distort words and actions and even attitudes between individuals so they become lethal weapons in the spiritual realm and very destructive to God's kingdom.

Things have been worked out between all concerned parties in this incident. We still have all of our instruments playing in the services, and there seems to be more harmony among our people. I think the congregation has learned a valuable lesson. Praise the Lord!

Sometimes what is said is spoken with the slightest inflection in the voice and can be misinterpreted by the hearer. When I lived in Phoenix, we had a man in our church (he has since died) who I very much appreciated. He was always with me in the sermon offering "Amen" and "Praise the Lord!" This was like adding gas to a flame for a preacher, and it encouraged me in my preaching! One day, I told him that I certainly appreciated his verbal support during my sermons. Satan immediately twisted the compliment that I was trying to share, and the man went from the church feeling that I had "talked down" to him. He said he would never attend our services again. He never did! I apologized, asked for forgiveness, pleaded in every way I knew how trying to clear this breach in our relationship. Nothing worked. I had been sincere in what I said—my motives were pure and right. He'd heard the same comment; only he interpreted it through demonic filters. Christians have to be so careful!

I need to mention that demons work really well at starting and feeding domestic quarrels. Again, words can be twisted. Voice intonation can be misinterpreted. Mouths can say one thing, and ears hear another. Demons are especially successful in their work if there's already stress in the marriage or in the home. Couples need to pray together and read God's Word together and be certain that they're communicating together. If there's a question about what has been said or the intent of what was just said, please learn to sit down together and discuss clearly what is being conveyed. A lot of homes would be much more peaceful if the couples would just make an effort to listen to what the other one is trying to say and not react to what they thought was said. The devil's demons will do what they can to inflame any situation!

Along with this, it should be mentioned that communication needs to be guarded between parents and children, brothers and sisters, and all who live within the home. If Satan can get everybody fighting and get everyone mad, he has defeated the home and compromised the family.

Listen, Satan and his cohorts will torment you in any way that he can. He wants to make your Christian walk miserable, and he wants to defeat you. He'll make you worry over needless things. He'll offer all kinds of reasons why you should get your feelings hurt and quit. He will harass you about your personal commitment to Jesus Christ. He will say that God doesn't love you, God doesn't answer prayer, or God is mad at you. He'll tell you that you have sinned so badly that God cannot ever forgive you. The lies just go on and on.

The fact is *they are lies! All lies!* Satan is a liar and the father of lies and can't tell the truth! Learn to discern who is talking to you. Satan accuses you of sinning but is never specific as to the charge. He makes you think you must do what you're going to do *now* because if you don't act now, it'll be too late. He doesn't offer any kind of answer for the dilemma—just a sense of panic and frustration. Satan is a cruel taskmaster for those people he has in bondage! He tries to bully and scare those who don't belong to him. Who would want to serve a master like that?

God works much more gently. He convicts our heart in such a way that we know and understand where the problem lies. We often are miserable because we're out of God's will, but God wants to forgive us and not just condemn us. John 3:17 says, "God sent not His Son into the world to condemn the world; but that the world through Him might be saved." God always shows us the path to take to restore fellowship with Him. God loves us! God coaxes us to Himself to give us eternal Life. God's way certainly is the best way! I want to be one of His children!

BEWARE OF FAMILIAR SPIRITS!

God's Word has some interesting things to say to us about "familiar spirits" and how we should avoid them. Listen to several scripture references from the King James Version:

> Regard not them that have familiar spirits, neither seek after wizards, to be defiled by them: I am the LORD your God. (Lev. 19:31)

> A man also or woman that hath a familiar spirit, or that is a wizard, shall surely be put to death; they shall stone them with stones: Their blood shall be upon them. (Lev. 20:27)

> And when they shall say unto you, Seek unto them that have familiar spirits, and unto wizards that peep, and that mutter: should not a people seek unto their God? For the living to the dead? (Isa. 8:19)

> For he shall give His angels charge over thee, to keep thee in all thy ways. They shall bear thee up in their hands, lest thou dash thy foot against a stone. (Ps. 91:11-12)

God's plan calls for ministry of the righteous by His angels. We each have "guardian angels" assigned to watch over and protect us. That is what Psalm 91:11-12 (quoted above) seems to indicate. From this scripture and others come the doctrine of "guardian angels." In Hebrews 1:14, we're told that angels are ministering spirits sent to the heirs of salvation: "Are they not all ministering spirits, sent forth to minister for them who shall be heirs of salvation?"

The *heirs of salvation* would be you and me and anyone who knows and claims Jesus Christ as his personal savior. The ministry of angels is for us and in our behalf.

74

Satan always tries to counterfeit or copy God's plan. He has no original thoughts of his own and is trying to take the place of God. Because Satan always attempts to counterfeit God, he also uses his fallen angels to carry out his program. Among these fallen angels (demons), we find a group called familiar spirits.

The word *familiar* comes from the same Latin word used for *family* and is used for that which is "known through constant association." This is usually in reference to people. The Bible clearly teaches that people and demons can associate. Only the disillusioned and ignorant Christians want to deny demonic existence. *The world knows they're there!*

Satan assigns one of his "familiar spirits" to a person or a family. This demon is to find out if that person or family is susceptible to spiritual things. If so, the demon starts the process of collecting a very intimate and detailed file of information on that person or family. Usually the demon will work on one person rather than a whole family.

In order to see how these familiar spirits work, we need to know something about them. Demonic activity is designed to harass, agitate, vex, overpower, and finally possess the person.

The familiar spirit on duty doesn't take possession of his victim. He works like a private detective would work—watching the person night and day, at play, at work, alone and with other people. By doing this, he can learn the most intimate details of the person's life.

Since the person cannot see him, a familiar spirit can remain undetected by the person whom he is watching.

He has many supernatural abilities, and all are used for deception. He never does anything good or constructive. Satan's forces are incapable of doing good and constructive things because they've sold out to evil and rebellion against God. That is why there is not "white magic" and "black magic" among witches. It is all "black magic," and its source is always evil! This is something that needs to be understood by people who have allowed a "spirit guide" into their lives and think that the "spirit guide" is their friend who they can trust and who will help them. That demon doesn't want to help—*he wants to destroy that person!* He'll tell all the lies that he needs to tell to get the job done! Some people rely upon the information that their "spirit guide" gives them as if it were the truth. *It is not!* Demons can't tell the truth because they are all liars just like Satan is a liar!

The familiar spirit collects all kinds of information: talents, resources, friends, neighbors, enemies, likes, dislikes, habits, mental abilities, educational abilities, the person's response to certain stimuli or different situations. It's the responsibility of this personal demon to know everything he can about the person he is watching. He literally must "get to know that person from A to Z."

In time, he learns exactly how his victim will respond to many kinds of circumstances and stimuli. He can actually figure out patterns of thought by using the power of suggestion. He will place a thought into the victim's mind and watch the reaction. The person will probably think the thought originated within himself and will, therefore, not feel threatened. This is Satan's superdisguise. He can place thoughts in our minds using the "I or me" format, and we don't recognize the source of the thought or idea.

I need to say very clearly that Satan and his demons cannot read your mind! Only God knows your innermost thoughts! Satan is not omniscient like God. He has to rely on educated guesswork. Therefore, if you want to pray to God in private, you may do so by thinking your prayer to Him but not speaking it aloud. God hears and knows our thoughts. Try these scriptures to understand what I am saying:

> And Jesus, knowing their thoughts said, Wherefore think ye evil in your hearts? (Matt. 9:4)

> And Jesus knew their thoughts, and said unto them, Every kingdom divided against itself is brought to desolation; and every city or house divided against itself shall not stand. (Matt. 12:25)

> For the Word of God is quick, and powerful, and sharper than any twoedged sword, piercing even to the dividing asunder of soul and spirit, and of the joints and morrow, and is a discerner of the thoughts and intents of the heart. (Heb. 4:12)

Satan and his demons can only guess what you're thinking. They can do this because they have knowledge of your lifestyle and how you've responded before to their power-of-suggestion stimuli.

To illustrate: I can know if I offer my daughters chocolate or boiled turnips that they'll choose the chocolate. I know their patterns. I know what they like and what they dislike.

Once a familiar spirit has learned the necessary information about a person and has completed his research, his assignment changes. He then begins to maneuver that person into the presence of a spiritualist medium. Mediums fall in to several categories. Not all of them hold séances where they try to communicate with the dead. They also include fortune-tellers, astrologers, magicians, sorcerers, witches, New Agers, clairvoyants, and so on. Their "talents" vary, but all have one thing in common: *all of them are possessed by familiar spirits, and what they do is strongly forbidden by God!*

> There shall not be found among you any one that maketh his son or his daughter to pass through the fire, or that useth divination, or an observer of times, or an enchanter, or a witch, or a charmer, or a consulter with familiar spirits, or a wizard, or a necromancer. For all that do these things are an abomination unto the lord: and because of these abominations the lord thy god shall drive them out from before thee. Thou shalt be perfect with the LORD thy God. (Deut. 18:10-13)

Also, refer back to Leviticus 19:31 and Leviticus 20:27, which were quoted at the beginning of this chapter.

A medium is a person who has literally been taken over and/or is possessed by a familiar spirit. We know of some of the more famous New Age "channelers" who are bringing society into contact with demons today. It's safe to assume they are demon possessed. But the truth is, all who are involved in these forms of forbidden activities are demonized: fortune-tellers, clairvoyants, astrologers, séance mediums, reincarnationists, New Age leaders—all are demonized!

Christians have absolutely no business playing around with any of these things! We cannot indulge in any of these activities without getting ourselves in a lot of danger and trouble.

Once the familiar spirit has maneuvered his person into the presence of a spiritualist medium, he is ready for the next step. He simply transfers the detailed information that he has collected about the person to the familiar spirit who possesses the medium. The demons have no trouble communicating with each other in the spirit world.

We know God can and does transmit information to His angels and His children—Satan does the same thing. A familiar spirit has no problem sharing his information with another spirit.

When the person comes into the presence of a medium, the familiar spirit living in and controlling the medium receives the information that has been collected on that person's life. Now he knows what approach to use to completely disarm his new victim.

I have a Christian friend who used to be one of the leading fortune-tellers in Las Vegas, Nevada. She told me that when she "read" somebody's fortune, she simply put into words the information that her demon had received from the other person's demon. It all seemed so mysterious! The medium simply received that information from the "familiar spirit" and used it to tell his or her new customer details that the unsuspecting person was certain nobody knew. The information revealed by the medium includes very personal and intimate details, which the victim is certain that no one else could possibly know.

"Wow! How could she know that? I haven't even told my family!"

The customer is hooked! He thinks, *I've never seen this person before. How could he (or she) have known so much about me?*

Interestingly enough, it's not always a professional fortune-teller that is used in this manner. Some people wouldn't think of going to a fortune-teller. Sometimes it's a person that crosses our path and seems to have a sixth sense about who we are and what we're going through. There is always a temptation to trust and confide in such a person because "he really understands me and knows where I am coming from." *Beware!* Don't "spill your guts" to just anyone. Be certain the person you're trusting and confiding in is a Christian and really has your and God's best interests in mind. I've had people come into my office who seemed to know many things about what I was going through and knew of the struggles of my life. When they won my confidence, they used private information that I'd entrusted to them to cause problems for me and the church. Most of the time, they took a part truth and twisted it into a whole lie. It's always hard to combat such lies when they come from a person who seems "to be in the know." I've found the best ones to confide in are God and my wife. If I need to talk further, I usually find a tree or a fence post to talk to. Somehow they keep secrets quite well! I suppose you could talk to a pet dog if he wagged his tail and not his tongue.

The medium and the controlling spirit will use only as much information as is necessary to captivate the person. Another visit is arranged.

At the next meeting, even more information is revealed—drawing the victim even farther into the snare. Once the victim has returned, the trap is shut with an announcement by the medium that his or her ability is God-given. This is designed to completely disarm the victim. This can happen even to pastors who should know better.

From this point on, the person is drawn into a very deep and destructive series of events, which can eventually lead to his becoming possessed by a demon.

The medium will speak of things no one else could possibly know or understand.

How did the medium get this information? It is through the transfer of information between the demon spirits. When a person tells you that "God has revealed these things to me," find out which god he's speaking about—the Christian's God doesn't gossip! God usually speaks directly to the individual through the Holy Spirit. It may be as the result of a sermon or a passage in the Bible, but God brings the conviction upon the human heart, and the person knows he is dealing with God. My God is capable of communicating with me when He wants to do so! I'm always suspicious when someone approaches me and says, "I have a message for you from God." I can hear God. He doesn't have to send someone who seems just a little off-the-wall.

I hope that you've seen some of how fortune-telling and the like activities work. Remember, Satan doesn't always use someone who claims to be a fortune-teller to do his bidding. Sometimes the person may seem like a very concerned friend. Pray that God will give you discernment in your dealings with people.

Another phenomenon that is coming to our society from the New Age movement is the teaching about *reincarnation*. Many people are confused today about this false teaching. The New Age movement is claiming that when we leave this life, we're recycled and come back in a new body for a new life. We have to do this hundreds of times until we finally get it right and work all of our "karma" out of our spirit. I read recently in some New Age literature that a soul has to be recycled at least 900 times over a period of one million years in order to reach nirvana. It made me tired just to think of it. I hope I have strength to live clear through this one lifetime!

The teaching of reincarnation is a stupid lie! It goes back to what the devil told Eve in the Genesis account of the fall, "You will not surely die!" It was a bold-faced lie then, and it's a bold-faced lie now! Hebrews 9:27 says, "It is appointed unto man once to die, but after this the judgment." The teaching of reincarnation is based on Hindu teachings. The big difference is that a Hindu might come back as a bug, a cow, or a blade of grass. The westerners like to think they'll always come back in a human form. You'd think that modern man would be smart enough not to buy into such a lie as reincarnation. But "scientists" have used hypnosis and other mind-altering techniques to "transport" people back to other "lifetimes." The information and details given in these sessions can be checked out and often seem quite accurate. How do you explain someone living today and knowing the details of a life lived long ago in a different place and time if they didn't live that life?

The operation of familiar spirits thoroughly explains the inner workings of reincarnation. It also explains what happens at séances where attempts are made to communicate with the dead who are now "on the other side." What takes place is actually the work of familiar spirits or demons, which studied the people in question. They can give details of someone's life from times past because they were there and saw what was going on—probably were involved in that life. They can reveal "memories" to a modern person about things that the person never experienced but doesn't know why they know so many details. They can impersonate a dead person at a séance because they know the details of that person's life. They know how the person spoke, and they have little trouble giving a convincing performance to gullible people seeking information that God doesn't want them to obtain. Remember, demons have been around for thousands of years, and we're not the first generation to have dealings with them. They know names and details from other generations and all periods of history.

Psychiatrists probe people's minds—many stories that are uncovered are simply amazing! It seems they have a breakthrough in answering questions about what happens after death. Yet it's the work of demons. Satan has little trouble outwitting the intellectual carnal mind! It is no problem for a demon to implant in somebody's mind certain information about a previous life of someone he has possessed. The dead person is not contacted and is not communicating during a séance. It's only a demon pretending to be "Uncle Harry" or "Aunt Mable." They must enjoy playing such a hoax on poor unsuspecting humans.

Reader, listen to me! Fortune-telling, séances, Ouija boards, horoscopes, tarot cards, and the like are not to be played with by Christians! God's people shouldn't even pretend about such things at parties or other activities. *Leave these things completely alone! They are deadly!* Read again Leviticus 20:27.

The Old Testament declares that those possessed by familiar spirits will be destroyed. God specifically identifies witches and wizards or warlocks—mediums! We don't stone them today because of the laws of our land, but they're still under a sentence of death. They'll be held responsible for their own destruction and death.

There is a growing fascination with angels today. Christian bookstores are full of books about angels and angelic encounters. Movies are being made about angels. Television programs feature information about angels. One program even offered to help you get in contact with your own guardian angel.

Be careful! Satan and his forces will come disguised as "an angel of light" (2 Cor. 11:14). As Christians, we have one focal point that we're to dwell upon and that is Jesus Christ! Even The Holy Spirit's main duty is to exalt Jesus. Don't get caught up in the angel movement that is going on currently. If you do encounter an angel, make him acknowledge who his master is. Not all angels come from God or from heaven! First John 4:2-3 tells us,

> Hereby know ye the Spirit of God: Every spirit that confesseth that Jesus Christ is come in the flesh is of God: And every spirit that confesseth not that Jesus Christ is come in the flesh is not of God: and this is that spirit of antichrist, whereof ye have heard that it should come; and even now already is it in the world.

Satan is having a heyday pushing demons pretending to be angels at society today.

Satan is a cruel taskmaster! After he has captured a person and has used him in every possible way and there is nothing left for him to do, he maneuvers that person to a place of certain destruction in the most hideous way. Satan doesn't love or even care about his followers. He promises them power, wealth, sex—whatever it takes to entice them to him. *He offers them death!* You can see it today in our society. People are deceived into demonic entrapment. Destruction is everywhere. Suicide, drug overdoses, murder, depression, stress, crime, violence, and whatever else offers destruction is all that Satan can bring to his disciples.

God has warned us all that we should not play around with familiar spirits. Review Leviticus 19:31.

Never in history has there been a more blatant display of the occult than there is today. Mediums, fortune-tellers, clairvoyants, astrologers, New Agers—our society is glutted with it all. God has forbidden such acts and warns us to stay clear of those who have familiar spirits. Too often, psychics, New Agers, and the like are invited by universities, business organizations, civic groups, and even churches to address people with their lies. Demonic-oriented people shouldn't be brought in to disturb the minds of literally thousands of men and women. These people aren't of God. They're demonized!

God said that they defile those who hear them. Every astrologer, clairvoyant, wizard, fortune-teller, magician, sorcerer, or medium that you listen to with your ears or read from with your eyes will defile you. They mislead, misguide, and confuse all who will listen to them!

*If you want direction for your life—**go to God!** He knows 100 percent what you should be and where you should be!*

Listen again to Isaiah 8:19:

> And when they shall say unto you, Seek unto them that have familiar spirits, and unto wizards that peep, and that mutter: should not a people seek unto their God? for the living to the dead?

Isaiah is saying when people invite you to indulge in these occult practices (including movies, personal-computer programs, horoscope columns, and so on), you're about to be trapped. Don't accept their invitation!

Tell them that you serve a God who knows all that you need to know about future events, and that you're perfectly satisfied with Him in your life.

The Word of God is so full of truth, so rich in blessings, and so complete that we don't need anything else!

The Holy Spirit gives us sound, healthy, and wholesome spiritual involvement. We don't need to involve ourselves with demons! Besides, we know *that Satan is a liar, and there is no truth in him!*

> Ye are of your father the Devil, and the lusts of your father ye will do. He was a murderer from the beginning, and abode not in the truth, because there is no truth in him. When he speaketh a lie, he speaketh of his own: for he is a liar, and the father of it. (John 8:44)

KNOW WITH WHOM YOU ARE DEALING!

Beloved, believe not every spirit, but try the spirits whether they are of God: because many false prophets are gone out into the world.

Hereby know ye the Spirit of God: Every spirit that confesseth that Jesus Christ is come in the flesh is of God:

And every spirit that confesseth not that Jesus Christ is come in the flesh is not of God: and this is that spirit of antichrist, whereof ye have heard that it should come; and even now already is it in the world.

Ye are of God, little children, and have overcome them: because greater is he that is in you, than he that is in the world.

—1 John 4:1-4

It's important that Christians learn to discern spirits. Too many Christians are being destroyed because they're not careful about what spirits they allow to control them. Today's Christians are so geared to high emotion and of "feeling good" that they've become perfect targets for demonic control. Not every spirit that brings a "euphoria" is from God. Learn to test the spirits—don't just accept them at face value. Meditation requiring the person to blank his mind is dangerous. As Christians, we're to be in control of our thoughts. This means we should never be hypnotized or asked to blank our minds or submit to any entity that wants to be our "spirit guide."

Many large corporations, businesses, police departments, and branches of the armed forces are training their executives and employees to get in contact with the "inner self" or "find the inner guidance in your being" or to seek "wisdom from your spirit guide." The method used is to picture yourself in some "secret secluded place." Through breathing techniques and letting the mind drift and float and imagining a sense of well-being, the person is placed in contact with some "superior being," be it called the "deeper self" or a "friend who wants to help you" or "your own spirit guide" or even "your own angel." The truth is that while the mind is left unguarded, a demon has come in masquerading as a friend and guide for your life. *He's no friend!* Untold agony has come to unsuspecting people trying to "get in touch with a higher being" or "get in touch with the inner self." The only safe one to be in touch with and give access to your mind is Jesus Christ. When you meditate on Christ and His Word, the Bible, you don't blank your mind; instead, you use your mind to think inspired thoughts.

I counseled with a lady in Arizona once, who'd been told that she would have a more meaningful prayer life if she would "visualize" Jesus as she prayed. She began to "conjure" up an image of Christ each time she prayed. It wasn't long before a demon began coming to her at these times of "prayer." He would tell her he was "Jesus." She let him take control of her mind, her spirit, and her body. She testified that she began to have a sexual relationship with this entity. She would stand up in church and say, "I know what it means to be the bride of Christ. I slept with Him last night." I would immediately tell her she was out of order and command her to sit down and be quiet. This was always a disruption to the worship service or to the Sunday school class if she was in Sunday school. The poor lady was tormented unmercifully. She spent much time in mental hospitals. Her marriage was a wreck. It all started when she tried to "visualize" Christ and, as a result, became vulnerable to demonic entry.

Be in control of your thoughts! You must someday account to God for every idle thought, every word, and every action (Heb. 4:12-13).

There are many dangerous areas that Christians need to watch. Sometimes the music we listen to can cause to have a "short circuit" in our thought processes and expose us to demonic entry. This is the case with some of the "rock-jungle beats" and the pieces that repeat a phrase over and over again. Unfortunately, some music known as Christian rock falls in to this category, but we will deal with Christian rock at another time.

The Psalmist hit the nail on the head for a Christian striving to please God:

> Let the words of my mouth, and the meditation of my heart, be acceptable in thy sight, O Lord, my strength and my redeemer. (Ps. 19:14)

A Christian should only expose his mind to things that will bring glory to Jesus Christ. If there's a question to what falls in that category, then I refer you to a phrase coined years ago, "When in doubt, leave it out." If you don't know what you're doing or thinking is pleasing to God, then don't do it or think it!

I'm also concerned about some of the activities happening in the "religious world" today. I have seen a group of preachers that invite people to become "giddy" and uncontrollable in response to their sermons. One fellow stands and gives one-liners, and the people lose control of themselves. They act drunk, they pass out on the floor, they have no control of their actions. The preacher passes this off as the "work of the Holy Spirit." Another group allows manifestations of all descriptions—crying, laughing, shaking, screaming, falling down, passing out—everything imaginable and says this is God working in the peoples' lives. It smacks demonic to me!

First Corinthians 14:33 says, "God is not the author of confusion, but of peace, as in all churches of the saints."

Something is dangerously wrong with today's brand of religious excitement. We must learn how to discern what spirits are among us. I believe God brings excitement and emotion to His people on occasion, but we need to be sure that what we're experiencing is from God and that we haven't opened the door to demons to counterfeit an experience we desire. Too often people seek a "gift" and not the "giver." Seek the giver—God and let Him decide what He wants to place in your life. A deep relationship with God doesn't come without prayer, scripture, and obedience to His will.

ANOINTING WITH OIL

Exodus 30:22-32 gives God's recipe for the preparation of a holy anointing oil. This oil was prepared especially to consecrate items and individuals involved in the worship of God. This anointing signified that these instruments and people were set aside for God's specific use. The area, tools, and people became holy unto the Lord!

Again, in Exodus 40:9-16, Moses was instructed to anoint the tabernacle, the instruments used in the tabernacle for sacrifice and worship, and Aaron and his sons with oil. This oil is a sign that these special things have been dedicated to God and set aside for God's holy use and man's worship of God. Oil is usually a symbol of the Holy Spirit in the Bible. It speaks of the fact that something has been consecrated to God.

James 5:14-15 tells us that if there are sick among us, the elders of the church should come and pray over him and anoint him with oil in the name of the Lord, and the prayer of faith will heal the sick, and the Lord shall raise him up.

In the scriptures that I've cited, oil is used to dedicate, purify, and perform God's will.

I use oil in spiritual warfare too. The scriptures used here and other scriptures support the use of oil in God's special warfare work. I am acquainted with several pastors and other people working in "deliverance ministries" that rely upon the use of oil. Probably the first time I became aware of the use of oil was when I was working so closely with Dr. Rebecca Brown. She used oil to provide safe havens from demonic attack, help in the healing of demonic wounds, consecrate areas for special spiritual work, and expel demonic entities from rooms and buildings. My first reaction was that it might border on superstition, but I noticed that others in spiritual warfare were using oil too. A Nazarene pastor in Idaho was anointing his property lines to ward off demonic attack on his church. A friend of mine in Renton, Washington, anointed his church buildings because his congregation had been plagued with a spirit of sexual promiscuity for years. Several former pastors of that church had succumbed to sexual compromise and were out of the ministry. After the anointing with oil and the reclamation of the facilities for God's work, the problem seemed to subside. Another pastor friend of mine living in Skamania County, Washington, anointed his church and grounds to combat demonic activity that had been occurring. He reported a lessening in the attacks.

I've personally seen how anointing with oil has yielded results in my ministry. I will mention a few incidents where God has honored and protected me and others of His people in a very specialized calling.

I use olive oil as my anointing oil. I buy the oil in large quantities, so I will have it on hand when I need it. Actually, I got in such heavy warfare in Phoenix, that I kept my oil in a quart-sized bottle with a squirt pump so I could reach those hard-to-get places that needed to be anointed in the buildings and on the church property. It made it easier to anoint property lines if the property was large in size. I heard a preacher say that he felt we should use three-in-one oil because God is three in one. I'm sure he was just enjoying his "sick humor."

Never let anointing with oil become a ritual with not much thought to it. It's a powerful weapon and shouldn't be taken casually. I don't anoint property or buildings unless God has nudged me to do so. Our relationship with God should never be rote, but always fresh and up-to-date. With these thoughts in mind, let's proceed to the how-tos of anointing.

Sometimes a person is aware that something is causing problems in a home or church that shouldn't be there. When my wife and I moved into the parsonage in Stevenson, Washington, we were aware that there was an unholy presence in the house. This seemed strange, especially since it's a parsonage, and usually only pastors and their families live in parsonages. I remembered that when we were helping people out of the occult in Phoenix, we often had strange entities in the home that had hitchhiked in with the witches or warlocks that we were ministering to on a regular basis. I'd have to anoint the house to drive them out. Something must have come into this parsonage in that same way. Sure enough! A woman used to live in the basement of the house that practiced witchcraft. She had placed a demon, which she called, Rebel, in the home to cause trouble for the pastors and their families who would reside here. What do you do to rid your home of an unwanted, obnoxious fiend? The first thing I do is to see if there is anything that would give the demon legal right to stay in the home and remove it entirely. These are such things as occult charms, jewelry, rock music, books and papers with pornography or occult materials, souvenirs that represent a heathen culture, publications from cultic religions, or anything that would be a compromise to God's standards must be gotten out of the house. These things allow Satan legal standing in the home because they belong to him and were brought into the home by a family member. Now I am ready for the oil.

I take one room at a time working from the rooms farthest from the main door and going toward the door. I anoint every window, door, and every opening to the outside (such as drains, vents, faucets, etc.). I anoint in the name of the Father, Son and Holy Spirit and rebuke and bind the demons in the name of Jesus Christ. I'm careful to leave the main door unanointed until I've anointed all other windows, doors, vents, etc. When everything is oiled, I command the demons to leave in the name of Jesus Christ. I have had times when the hair on the back of my neck stood straight up, and I sensed that the demons were resisting the command to leave. Don't fear this because they have no power to stand against a direct command from God or one of His children doing His work. I then ask God to usher anything out of the room that I might've missed. Then, and only then, I anoint the main door and seal it calling on the blood of Christ. I don't want to seal the room until I've ordered the demons out in the name of Jesus Christ. I don't want to trap them in the room because they do not want to cross an anointed doorway. I have had witches panic when they realized a room had been anointed. I repeat these steps in each room until I've cleansed the whole house. Finally, I am at the main entrance of the home where I once again cast out the demons in Christ's name. Again, I ask God to usher away anything that shouldn't be in a Christian home, and I seal that door too.

People ask, "How often should you repeat this process?" I believe God will let you know when it is time to do it again. He knows when and if the "seal" has been broken.

I work the same way in the church building. Sometimes God will impress me that it's time to anoint the church again. If I do what He suggests, the services that week usually are blessed and rewarding. If I choose to put off doing what He has asked me to do, invariably there will be confusion, turmoil, and frustration in the service. I will be on my face before God, apologizing for not doing what I knew I should've done. For some reason the devil makes anointing a church or a home seem like a real chore that you almost dread to do and want to put off until another time.

In Phoenix, I had a youth center called the Fishing Hole. We were open Friday afternoons and evenings. One year, we averaged 255 young people every week. Our high attendance was 355. Needless to say, we had all kinds of problems coming onto the church property on a regular basis. I had to keep the property anointed at all times just to maintain a semblance of peace. There was a public school across the street from our church and troublemakers seemed to congregate there to plan mischief that they could do against our program and kids. I got into the habit of anointing the school parking lot when I'd anoint the church property. This was quite a chore because the church grounds were a little over five acres, and the school parking lot was at least two acres. That's when I started using the squirt bottle in earnest. One night, 135 rowdy teens gathered on the school parking lot. They proclaimed themselves Satanists and said they were going to stop the good that we were doing and prove to everyone that Satan rules. I took my bottle and anointed the grounds and the parking lot and within minutes, all but five of the "witches" had gone away.

Another time, a drug dealer set up business in the parking lot at the school with the intent to sell drugs to my kids. I told him to move on, or I'd call the police. He told me it was public property, and he would stay, and if I caused him any problems, he'd see that I paid dearly for my trouble. "He had a lot of friends that knew how to hurt people bad." He said I would be very sorry if I didn't mind my own business. The thing was—I was minding my business! I walked past his car and began to anoint the parking lot. By the time I'd finished, he'd packed his things, slammed the car trunk, and sped away into the night. *It works!*

On another occasion, I received word on a Sunday afternoon that a known witch was planning to come to service that evening and break up our worship. I anointed the church parking lots and entryways and asked God for special help. She did show up, but when she crossed the property line, she got so sick she began to vomit violently. She had to be helped to her home. *Praise God!*

On another occasion, an occult couple wanted to cause problems in my church. They came just before service on a Sunday evening demanding to see me. I told them they would have to wait until after service. The sanctuary had been anointed, and they refused to come in to the service. They waited in the foyer during the entire service. Just before the evening service, I managed to slip to my office and anoint it with oil in the name of Jesus Christ. When we finally went to the office after the service, they could not remember why they wanted to confront and attack me. They left in a confused state and never came to cause me grief again.

A New Age bookstore was located less than half a mile from our church. The proprietor was recognized as a leading psychic in Phoenix. In fact, she was often interviewed on local radio talk shows about her abilities and New

Age insights. She was a witch. She headed up a coven of witches in the area. Because of the kind of work that we were doing, our church became a target for all kinds of occult, hexes, and spells. I'd often find pentagrams, parts of dead animals, or messages written in blood on the property. I'd anoint these things and pray for safety for our people. One night my youngest daughter, Kim, and I went to the witch's store. It was closed. We anointed the front door with oil in the name of Jesus Christ and asked the Lord to control who went into and out of that door. We asked God to curtail the activities that were coming from that place. Within five weeks, the store closed, and the witch moved her merchandise to another location seven miles away.

Anointing items that Satan can use for his purposes works too. Of course, if you have something that belongs to you and isn't compatible with your Christian witness, you must get rid of it. But what if the item belongs to someone else and you don't have the right to dispose of it? One of the ladies in my church had a teenage son who was into heavy rock music. She had told him "get rid of that junk!" He decided that he didn't have to get rid of it. He was big and in his late teens—she didn't know how to handle his rebellious attitude. She went in to his room while he was away. She anointed the tape player he used to play the evil music. Later, he told her that his player would no longer play his kind of music, but it had no problem playing Christian music and other nonoffensive tapes. I don't know if he ever figured out what had happened, but the mother and I knew.

I could go on relating many more occurrences that happened. I have several stories to tell from the area where I live now, but you have the idea. Anointing works. Be certain if you get into spiritual warfare to remember what a powerful weapon your oil bottle can be. Of course the oil has no power of its own, but the Holy Spirit certainly does! He is God, and His power is second to none in the universe! God has inspired me to use oil in my deliverance ministry, and it certainly has been a valuable tool.

THE ARMOR OF GOD

Finally, my brethren, be strong in the Lord, and in the power of his might.

Put on the whole armour of God, that ye may be able to stand against the wiles of the devil.

For we wrestle not against flesh and blood, but against principalities, against powers, against the rulers of the darkness of this world, against spiritual wickedness in high places.

Wherefore take unto you the whole armour of God, that ye may be able to withstand in the evil day, and having done all, to stand.

Stand therefore, having your loins girt about with truth, and having on the breastplate of righteousness;

And your feet shod with the preparation of the gospel of peace;

Above all, taking the shield of faith, wherewith ye shall be able to quench all the fiery darts of the wicked.

And take the helmet of salvation, and the sword of the Spirit, which is the word of God:

Praying always with all prayer and supplication in the Spirit, and watching thereunto with all perseverance and supplication for all saints;

And for me, that utterance may be given unto me, that I may open my mouth boldly, to make known the mystery of the gospel,

For which I am an ambassador in bonds: that therein I may speak boldly, as I ought to speak.

—Ephesians 6:10-20

If a person is involved in spiritual warfare, he'd better learn about "the armor of God." Too many people think this is just figurative. They think Paul was just using symbolism when he wrote this passage.

Paul wasn't using symbolism. He was describing literal spiritual armor that the Christians had better learn how to use if he wants to stand against the attacks of the devil. We need to memorize this passage and make a habit of asking God to dress us in our armor everyday.

Sooner or later, every Christian is going to find that the Christian life is a battleground. The enemy we face is much stronger than we are in our own power. It's only through Jesus Christ that we can face the tremendous opposition that we experience as the battle rages. We can come through victoriously, but it's not our strength or power, but Christ's strength that brings us to victory! Jesus earned that victory over Satan through the atonement! It's His victory that we enjoy. He is willing to share His victory with us, His Children! "In other words, as believers, we do not fight for victory—we fight from victory! The Spirit of God enables us, by faith, to appropriate Christ's victory for ourselves."[11]

According to Ephesians 6:12, the enemy is organized like a military army with ranks and levels of responsibility. This is a definite army of demonic creatures that work with Satan and follow his orders in his vicious attacks against the saints. We're in a spiritual battle whether we like it or not! We can ignore Satan and his forces all that we want, but he still isn't going to go away! People often say, "If we don't bother the devil, he probably won't bother us. Just leave him alone, and he'll leave us alone." Nothing could be further from the truth! If Satan is leaving you alone, it's probably because you belong to him already, and you don't pose a threat to his program! If you've identified with Jesus Christ, and He is your personal Savior and Lord, then you can expect to be challenged, plagued, accused, and attacked by satanic forces all the way to heaven's pearly gates!

---

[11]   Warren W. Wiersbe, *The Bible Exposition Commentary*, Vol. 2, (1993) Victor Books, Wheaton, Illinois, p. 57

We need to be aware of the enemy's forces if we plan to live our Christian life victoriously. The intelligence corps plays an important part in warfare because if makes it possible for the officers to know and understand the enemy. "Unless we know who the enemy is, where he is, and what he can do, we have a difficult time defeating him."[12] Not only in the sixth chapter of Ephesians but throughout the whole Bible, God tells us about our enemy. There really is no reason for us to be caught off guard!

In high school ROTC, we were taught the only reason for casualties on the battlefield was carelessness. Someone wasn't doing his job or became careless in some way. The same holds true on the spiritual battlefield.

Satan is the leader of the enemy forces. He has many different names. "Devil" means "accuser" because he accuses God's people day and night before the throne of God (Rev. 12:7-11). "Satan" means "adversary" because he is the enemy of God. He's also called the tempter (Matt. 4:3) and the murderer and the liar (John 8:44). He is compared to a lion in 1 Peter 5:8, a serpent in Genesis 3:1 and Revelation 12:9, and an angel of light in 2 Corinthians 11:13-15, as well as "the god of this world" in 2 Corinthians 4:4."[13]

Paul called Satan's army "principalities . . . powers . . . rulers . . . spiritual wickedness in high places."[14] Evidently, demonic forces are divided into different assignments. Some oversee the darkness and evil in the various geographical areas of the world. Some are assigned to be over cities and towns; some are assigned certain buildings and organizations. Some are the familiar spirits that work with families or one-on-one with individuals.

The important thing that we must understand is that our battle is not against human beings. It's against spiritual powers. We only waste our time when we fight people. We must fight the devil who wants to control people and make them strike out against the work of God.

Satan is a strong enemy! He isn't a cartoon character in long red underwear, wearing horns, and carrying a pitchfork. He is second only to the Godhead in the universe. We need the power of God to be able to stand against him. "Never underestimate the power of the devil. He is not compared to a lion and a dragon just for fun! The Book of Job tells us what his power can do to a man's body, home, wealth, and friends."[15]

---

[12]   Wiersbe, Ibid. P. 58
[13]   Wiersbe, Ibid. p. 58
[14]   Ephesians 6:12 KJV
[15]   Wiersbe, Ibid. p. 59

Jesus said Satan is a thief who comes "to steal and to kill and to destroy" (John 10:10). Satan isn't only strong, but he is crafty and subtle. We can't afford to be "ignorant of his devices" (2 Cor. 2:11).

I have good news for you! By keeping yourself "strong in the Lord," that is, equipping yourself with God's armor, you can successfully win the fight against the forces of evil. This is Paul's assurance. When we have on the armor of God, we are invincible against the attacks of Satan! Remember, it's through Christ's power and strength and not through our own merit that we have victory.

Well, how do you combat such an evil force as Satan and his demonic cronies? The Bible instructs us to pray to the Father, through the Son, and in the Holy Spirit. Romans 8:26-27 says that only in the Spirit's power can we pray in the will of God. If we're not in the will of God, our prayers are selfish and not in accordance to God's plan. We must be people of prayer if we're going to impact the powers of evil! Today there's such an absence of spiritual prowess that Satan is having a heyday as he runs rampant through society. We mourn, "Why are times so evil? What's gone wrong with our society? Where is the old-time power in the blood of Jesus Christ?"

There is *still power in the blood of Jesus Christ!* The saints aren't tapping that power because we hardly ever really pray. The result is we're getting "creamed," and we're losing a whole generation of young people that will wind up in hell because of our neglect. We've gotten too busy with our TVs, PCs, CDs, DVDs, communication devices, fancy homes, automobiles, and all the state-of-the-art conveniences of this generation. We really think we have no time for old-time intercessory prayer. The *power is still available* for the saints, but the saints are no longer *available for the power!* God help us to wake up soon before it's too late to snatch more people from Satan's clutches!

Christians are supposed to *persevere.* That simply means *to stick to it and not to quit!* Don't give up at the slightest discouragement that Satan puts in your path but be determined to see the battle through to the end! *Keep on praying!* Perseverance in prayer isn't trying to plead your case before God to change His mind. It's not twisting God's arm until He finally gives you your way. Instead, it is to be so burdened and have such concern that we can't rest until we have God's answer. Prayer isn't trying to get our will done in heaven. It's allowing God's will to be done here on earth.

Usually, we quit praying just short of the victory. Too often our prayer life runs similar to an story that I read in my e-mail entitled "Hold the

Line." A woman telephoned the manager of a large opera house and told him she'd lost a valuable diamond pin the night before at the concert. The man asked her to hold the line. A search was made, and the brooch was found; but when he got back to the phone, the woman had hung up. He waited for her to call again, and even put a notice in the paper, but he heard nothing further. What a strange and foolish person, we say, but isn't this the way some of us pray? We tell the Lord all about our needs, but then fail to "hold the line." The result is that we miss the joy of answered prayer and the thrill and reward of a persistent faith.

Keep praying until you know that God has stopped you or answered you. Just about the time you feel like quitting is the time that God will answer you. The problem is, however, that most of us don't understand what it means to endure in prayer today. It's not all that convenient, and it requires time and effort, and we're into convenience and time-savers! We don't want to put ourselves out for anything, and we certainly don't want to waste too much time on spiritual matters when there are so many other things crying for our attention in today's world.

Sometimes we feel that it isn't worth the effort to pray for a revival because we're probably the only church or people who want one (if it isn't too costly!). We are not fighting alone! There are other Christians joining with us. Jesus Christ is interceding for us. God is standing with us giving us strength and encouragement. But nothing is going to happen at all if we do not pray!

I hope that I've established the fact that we must pray. We now need to look at the armor that is provided for us according to Ephesians 6:10-18. We're told to "put on the whole armor of God." All the pieces are vitally important to our survival! Leaving any piece of our armor off will make us vulnerable to demonic attack.

We should note that "the order in which the pieces of armor are described is the order in which the soldier would put them on. Piece by piece Paul mentions the various parts of the military suit and applies each one to some aspect of Christian preparation for victorious living."[16]

The first piece of armor is the "truth" (Eph. 6:14). This will serve as the belt that holds everything together. We're instructed to stand, "having your loins girt about with *truth*." The free-flowing clothing of the East made it imperative for a soldier to fasten a belt around his waist in order to control the floppy tunic and hold it tightly to his body. This would enhance his

---

[16]   *Beacon Bible Commentary*, Beacon Hill Press of Kansas City (1965), p. 262

ability to move freely. The freedom of movement probably would keep him from defeat and death in the many tight places where he would find himself in battle. The belt also gave him a place to carry his sword. Other pieces of armor might even have been fastened to this belt.

This belt of truth in the Christian armor is faith and stability in God. Jesus said that He was "the way, the truth, and the life" (John 14:6). Over and over again, Paul said that the Word of God was truth. When we put on the belt of truth, we are standing on the Word of God with our faith totally in Christ Jesus. No matter what lies Satan tells to us or about us, we can stand firm on God's truth and will not be shaken. We have an anchor! It is truth. It is Jesus!

I'm so glad that I've built my ministry on truth. One time, in the heat of spiritual battle, a woman leveled accusations at me about a moral issue. Because I hadn't ever been deceitful in my relationship to my wife or to the church, nobody believed what she was saying, and the crisis passed leaving me unscathed. We need to put on truth—to stand for truth—and trust in our Savior, Jesus Christ, the one who is truth! His truth must become an everyday way of life! Ask God each day to put on you your "belt of truth."

The second piece of armor is "the breastplate of righteousness." The breastplate protected the chest and vital organs of the soldier. It was a means to bounce an arrow or an enemy sword away rather than have it penetrate the body and injure or kill the warrior. We're under attack constantly. Satan is trying to inflict a mortal wound into our spiritual relationship with God and, thus, destroy us as warriors and champions of the Lord.

In a society where lies, deceit, and cheating seem to be commonplace and even the expected mode of life, we need to stand forth in *God's righteousness and purity. Righteousness* isn't something we learn or acquire through practice; it's what we become through a close walk with Jesus Christ. "It is the life of purity and rectitude which the new relationship with God creates. Just as Truth has a subjective dimension, so with righteousness."[17] When a person is righteous, he is above suspicion. We can't always defend ourselves adequately with words against accusations, which arise, but our good exemplary life can be the testimony for the kind of individual that we really are. It's been said, "Right relationships are the soil in which the reward of righteousness can grow. And the only people who can sow these seeds, and who will reap the reward, are those whose life work it has been to produce such right relationships."[18]

---

[17]   Ibid., p. 263
[18]   William Barclay, *The Letter From James,*

The Christian must always be dressed in the breastplate of righteousness! Satan's fiery darts of lies and accusations will not so easily penetrate and destroy us if we're living righteously. We'll recognize his attempts to make us fall morally if we're living uncompromisingly *righteous* lives. We'll know how to "resist" his suggestions that are designed to destroy us. Ask God to put this vital piece of armor on you everyday! To yield to sin will make you vulnerable to Satan! He can't defeat you if you're living a *righteous life* in Christ Jesus. He doesn't need to defeat you if you're not up-to-date with Christ because you are already defeated spiritually. If God is pointing out sin in your life, take time to confess it now and get in a right standing with Him (1 John 1:9).

I spend time searching my heart and motives before I go into a "deliverance" to make certain that I have no unrighteous acts or motives in my life that haven't been confessed and forsaken. These sins might disqualify me from being used of God. If a demon can detect an area of hypocrisy, a "chink in my breastplate of righteousness," he will not heed me because he doesn't have to obey my commands in Jesus's name. If I'm regarding sin in my life and I'm not a true representative of Jesus Christ, I have no legal authority to command a demon to release an individual and evacuate that life. Actually, I have no authority to use the powerful name of Jesus if I'm in rebellion against Him. This isn't a game this is real! We're not just dealing with small issues—we're dealing with eternal issues, and we must be sensitive to that fact. Again, a good example of what can happen if a person isn't on top spiritually is found in the story of the seven sons of Sceva. They thought it would be a neat experience to cast demons out of a person. They forgot some vitally important preparation that they needed to do—that was having a personal relationship with Christ. Read about it in Acts 19:14-17. Deliverance isn't something to be too casual about.

The next item of armor involves having "your feet shod with the preparation of the gospel of peace" (Eph. 6:15). You're not going to do much in the way of success if your feet hurt! You need to have footwear that will enhance your ability to perform. The military sandals in Paul's day were made to protect the feet and to help the soldier to keep his balance in rough places. They also were designed for quick, sure footed movements. We, as Christians, must also have solid footing in our service to Christ! When we take a stand for Jesus and against the evil in this world today, we must know our footing is trustworthy.

The military shoes were designed to protect the feet from sharp sticks and stones or pieces of iron that were placed in the way to puncture the feet and from traps that could injure and cripple the soldier and make him unfit to march. Satan has set a lot of traps for our feet too. He hopes to make us unfit to march in Christ's Army by disqualifying us through temptations and snares designed to cause us to fall. We need to walk day by day in fellowship with our Lord. If temptation's snare snags us, we need to immediately turn to Jesus in repentance and get back into rank as His soldier. Ask Jesus to put His sandals on your feet today so that you may better stand against the enemy for Him.

Sometimes we do take a misstep, but our *sanctification* is determined by how long it takes us to come back to the Savior for reinstatement. If you do fall, get up quickly! It's not the fact that you went down that is so important, but it's the fact that you didn't stay down defeated. Always get up one more time when you fall down. This is a good lesson to learn in every aspect of life. When I was sixteen years old, I had an old Harley-Davidson motorcycle. I was riding it in the mountains near my home. I was with a friend. I took an awful spill and felt like I was hurt pretty badly. I asked my friend to take me home on his motorcycle, and we could bring a truck back to get my bike. He wouldn't give me a ride home. He told me to get up and get back on the motorcycle, or else I'd never ride it again because I'd be afraid. He was right! Finally, I got back on. I rode very carefully back to my home. But I did ride! I've been riding ever since and have enjoyed the sport. Think of what I would've missed had I just quit! I have been down several times since, but I always get back up and get back on the bike. I have still gotten back on one more time than I have fallen off, and I still enjoy riding.

So Satan defeated you in some circumstance somewhere! Big deal! Don't lie there and whimper like a boob! Get up! Put your shoes back on, and do something for Jesus! The Christian life is exciting if we'll let it be. It's always a challenge, and what a sense of accomplishment when we don't let the devil get the upper hand, but we get back up and destroy his plans instead! Haw! Haw! Praise God! I know that God must get a thrill when He sees us use His armor correctly!

No suit of Christian armor would be complete without the "shield of faith." (Eph. 6:16). The Roman military shield was a large oblong shield, which was part of the equipment used when the battle was severe. This wasn't just a decorative item but was very functional for protection. It was carved from wood and was covered with thick leather to stop and quench the fiery arrows shot by the enemy. It was long enough and wide enough to protect the entire body when the soldier crouched behind it. Often soldiers would stand side by side and create a wall of protection as they would hold their shields together. This would create a fortified protection that the enemy would have a rough time penetrating.

The heavily armed Christian warrior carries a shield of faith. Probably this is more necessary than any of the other parts of the armor though all are necessary! Faith is what we must have in the hour of temptation. The breastplate protects the vitals, but with the shield, we can turn every way. We can ward off attack from every direction. We're to be fully persuaded of the truth of God's promises in the face of any severe attack. Faith helps us stand steady when it looks like everything is falling apart, and defeat and disappointment are all we will have. We know faith will take us through and that ultimately, if we keep our trust and faith in God, we'll see victory! God hasn't, doesn't, and won't ever desert us in the face of the enemy and of trouble. With my shield of faith in the enemy's face, I cannot be defeated! Think of the things Christians could accomplish for Christ if we would put our shields together and work in a united cause for Him.

I said at the beginning of this chapter that people don't understand that the armor of God is literal and not just figurative. I want to illustrate what I mean. Dr. Rebecca Brown introduced me to a girl who had been raised to be a "breeder" in a coven of witches. That means she was supposed to have as many children as she could for the sake of human sacrifice. She'd been mistreated and abused all of her life. She was a pathetic individual because of this abuse. She conceived and had ten babies. Nine of them had been sacrificed. (I know that information like this is offensive to many readers, but the fact is that this happens). Finally, she was able to escape from the coven, and she accepted Jesus Christ as her personal savior. She was trying, with the help of some of my Christian friends, to get her life put back in some semblance of order but was having a tough time dealing with the pain and scars that the satanic abuse had left. One day, she was in a shopping mall in California. Two of the former tormentors from the coven that she had serviced saw her. They were "hell's-angels" type and mentality. She tried to avoid them and hide, but they'd already seen her. They came over to her and began to threaten her with violence. They said they were going to take her back to the coven. She panicked at the thought! What could she do? Suddenly, God reminded her of her "shield of faith." He'd protect her now if she would trust Him. She looked at these two big, ugly guys and said, "I am not going to go with you because I am going to raise my shield of faith, and God will protect me." With that, she outlined with her finger the dimensions of a shield, and she stood there behind it as if she were actually holding something. The two characters started to laugh, but suddenly looked up, and their mirth turned to panic. They took off running down the corridor of the mall like the death angel himself was after them. She didn't know what they had seen, but God must've revealed something more to them than just a frightened meek ninety-five-pound lady scared almost out of her wits. She did know that God had protected her when she used her shield of faith.

I had a personal experience along this line when I lived in Phoenix, Arizona. My daughter Kim and I were taking an evening stroll trying to cool down after a very hot day. We were talking and enjoying each other's company. As we passed a wooden fence, we heard a terrible commotion going on the other side of the fence. A big dog had heard us and was trying to get out and attack us. We could see him through a crack in the fence where a board was missing. He was big and as vicious looking as any dog that I'd ever seen. He seemed angry! Suddenly, the fence broke, and we were standing face-to-face with that ugly snarling dog. I could see the hatred in his eyes, the length of his yellow fangs, and the immense size of the animal. Kim and I were in trouble! Neither one of us could've defended ourselves against such a brute without massive injury. Suddenly, I rebuked and bound that dog in the name of Jesus Christ. I raised my "shield." The dog immediately changed direction (he was charging straight at us). He did a fast 180-degree turn and ran down the street with his tail tucked yipping like he'd been hurt. Kim and I had never seen anything like that before. We knew God had protected us from harm. The dog's owner came out of the yard, angry that we'd chased her monstrous mutt away. We just laughed and praised God that the dog had to look elsewhere for supper!

The shield of faith is a real and literal item in God's equipment for spiritual warfare. Learn to use it. Ask God to supply you with that shield each day. Learn that with your faith in an Almighty God; nothing can defeat you. "If God be for us, who can stand against us?" God is the master and controller of any circumstance. You can depend upon Him!

How could you go into combat and avoid head injury without a sturdy helmet? You couldn't! God's provided a helmet for His warriors. Ours is called the "helmet of salvation." The helmet secures the head. After putting on the other pieces of armor, the soldier received his helmet from his attendant. Now there'd be less chance for his skull to be crushed by a sword, battle-ax, or missile.

Our helmet of salvation is more than just great confidence that God has power to save. It seems to be more of a symbol of the protection that God's salvation assures. If a soldier goes into battle out of step with God, he has no guarantee of protection. If he is in a proper relationship with God, he'll be "more than conqueror." God takes care of His own people.

Christians spend too much time worrying that Satan is going to defeat or destroy them. Satan can't do to us anything that the permissive will of God will not allow. If we do go through times of trial and hardship, we can be rest assured that God will strengthen us and help us. He will allow hard places to develop our strength and usefulness for Him. He has promised in 1 Corinthians 10:13, "There hath no temptation taken you but such as is common to man: but God is faithful, who will not suffer you to be tempted above that ye are able; but will with the temptation also make a way to escape, that ye may be able to bear it." When we come through hard places successfully, it matures us in our Christian walk. Hard places can either make us better or bitter depending on how we let God minister to us through them.

My helmet of salvation allows me to trust God now and in the future for all my needs. The late Rev. Prescott Beals, veteran missionary in the Church of the Nazarene and one of my personal friends, used to say, "We are immortal as long as God has work for us to do! When our work is finished, we don't want to stay here anyhow!" He was right! I don't have time to worry about what Satan might do to me or my loved ones. I must do the work of Jesus who has called me. There's a battle out there that must be fought and won. With my helmet of salvation in place, I'm assured of the final outcome. I can say with the psalmist, "I will both lay me down in peace, and sleep: for thou, LORD, only makest me to dwell in safety" (Ps. 4:8).

To illustrate how literal the helmet of salvation is, I want to share some personal experiences. I usually ask God to dress me in my armor before I go into a deliverance situation. I want to be properly attired before facing off with any demons. I noticed that when I first began this ministry that I often would have to go to the dentist the next day after a conflict. This was especially true if I had to deal with a spirit guide. Somehow, I always seemed to get hit in the face. I've had seven root canals and a whole lot of other painful and expensive work done in my mouth. I even had to have one root canal redone because it flared and abscessed after a deliverance. My dentist would ask me when I came in, "Well, what have you been doing now?" One day, as I was preparing for a deliverance conflict, I asked God if He would put a face guard on my helmet of salvation. It sounds funny, but I didn't have to go to the dentist the next morning!

There's a warlock in the town where I used to live. He knew who I was and what I did. He was constantly trying to "put things on me." I noticed that when I met him in the store or in a restaurant that I would soon have a massive headache that would last the rest of the day. Sometimes it was so bad that I'd get sick and vomit. I began asking God to put my helmet of salvation on me when I'd see him coming. I no longer had the drastic headaches after the encounters with this individual. I have many other illustrations concerning this fellow, but that will be in another book someday.

So far, the armor has been for defense to protect us from the attack of Satan. Now we will look at the offensive weapon—the "sword of the Spirit" (Eph. 6:17).

The Roman soldier would've been helpless without his sword. He'd use his sword to slash his way through the enemy ranks. The enemy would fold in front of his sharpened blade. Our sword of the Spirit that we use to slash away demonic forces and Satan himself is the Word of God! It's so very important to read, memorize, and know the Word of God! When Jesus was under attack from Satan, He quoted scripture, and Jesus stood firm while Satan fled. Our very authority for spiritual warfare comes through the shed blood of Jesus Christ and our knowledge of the divine Word of God.

When I was a boy, my grandmother would instruct me on the importance of knowing the scriptures and being able to tell Satan how Jesus has given me victory through God's Word. She'd say to me, "Billy, just plea the blood! Satan cannot stand it when you plea the blood." I've found it's true! Satan can't stand up against the wonderful words of life!

In one terrific battle several years ago, I learned the power of the Bible. I'd been working with a young man who had been very involved with the martial arts and several other aspects of the occult. I was trying to teach him how to "stand." Satan's forces were attacking him and trying to discourage him and destroy his newly found Christian faith. I came out my door one morning to find this young man's truck parked at our front curb. He was inside the cab and was unconscious. Evidently, he'd been in a tremendous battle and had tried to make it to my house for help. He had only gotten to our front yard. I carried him inside the house, rebuking, and binding the evil spirits that were oppressing him in the name of Jesus Christ. Once inside, I grabbed my Bible and began reading the last three chapters of the book of Revelation to the demonic forces. I reminded them of their future in hell and told them that what I was reading was about their end that was soon to come. The fellow regained consciousness before I had read very many verses. Satan's forces can't stand to hear the Word of God. They know they've lost the battle and will spend eternity in hell. They won't be ruling like Satan likes to brag to his crowd, but they'll be in torment forever and forever.

All the other pieces of armor mentioned in this list are defensive in nature. They're designed to help the Christian to stand. But the sword of the Spirit is for offensive warfare. We're not to sit and watch the battle. It's not a spectator sport. We're to pick up our swords, shield in one hand, and sword in the other, and aggressively go and claim territory for our Lord.

When we have God's Word, we can destroy doubts and fears. We can overcome temptations. We can stand in the heat of battle. We can rescue souls from Satan's bondage. We can inflict mortal wounds upon our enemy! Praise God! Let's do it!

Keep strong in prayer, memorize and use God's Word, and give the devil the thrashing he deserves in the name of Jesus Christ! Above all, remember to keep your armor on at all times!

OBEDIENCE IS
THE BOTTOM LINE!

People tell me they'd like to get into a deliverance ministry. Somehow, many individuals have the idea they could be a spiritual Agent 007 working for the forces of God. Too many people want the "sense of power" they imagine would come by casting out demons. They like to think they'd receive special recognition for their godly performance. They'd be the center of attention in religious circles.

Let me warn you: those are the same motives that drive the Satanist in his quest for power and recognition. Jesus will never honor that attitude with His blessing. He said in Luke 10:19-20, "Behold, I give unto you power to tread on serpents and scorpions and over all the power of the enemy: and nothing shall by any means hurt you. Notwithstanding in this rejoice not, that the spirits are subject unto you; but rather rejoice, because your names are written in Heaven." Whatever power we may have isn't our power but His power. He should always get the glory for any victory that is won! We ought to just be hilarious that our names are written in the book of life and that we are adopted into His family!

Recently, a fellow was bragging to me that he was a "captain" in God's spiritual army, and demons had to submit to his authority. He said demons would quake when they saw him coming. I don't know who told him his rank! I do know that he'd better be careful because demons don't submit to humans be they captains or generals. Demons submit to the name and authority of Jesus Christ! This gentleman went on to tell me that I was just a sergeant. It doesn't matter if I'm just a private! That's God's business! My business is to serve and glorify my master and Lord! James and John got reprimanded when they thought too highly of themselves that time they came with their mother to ask Jesus if they could sit on thrones to the right and left of His throne in His kingdom.

King Saul got too "big for his breaches" and overstepped his authority. God had instructed him in 1 Samuel 15 to destroy all the Amalekites, the enemies of Israel, including their King, Agag. He was supposed to see that all of their property and livestock were utterly destroyed. "But Saul and the people spared Agag, and the best of the sheep, and of the oxen, and of the fatlings, and the lambs, and all that was good, and would not utterly destroy them" (1 Sam. 15:9).

Samuel was late getting to his appointment with Saul and the people. When he arrived, he heard the cows and the sheep and saw King Agag—still alive! He asked Saul what this meant. Saul said they'd decided to save the best of the livestock to sacrifice to God. (This was a last-ditch effort on Saul's part to save his own bacon because he and the people really wanted this plunder for themselves.)

Samuel was irate at Saul's disobedience to the clear command of God. He said, "Hath the LORD as great delight in burnt offerings and sacrifices, as in obeying the voice of the LORD? Behold, to obey is better than sacrifice, and to hearken than the fat of rams" (1 Sam. 15:22). Saul would've been better off just to obey what God had told him to do. Because of his disobedience, he lost the kingdom of Israel to his family line and lost God's blessing upon his own life.

It would be easy to criticize Saul for his effort to substitute sacrifice for obedience, but don't we often try the same thing? Don't we sometimes try to bargain with God rather than do what He's instructed us to do? Our sacrifices won't please Him if we're not obeying Him. Nothing short of total obedience will satisfy our holy God.

Jesus said, "If ye love me, keep my commandments" (John 14:15). It's that simple! If you love Jesus, you'll do what He says. We would rather volunteer for the "dangerous duties" or sacrifice and be "martyrs" for His cause or do something heroic that nobody else has done because that will draw attention to ourselves. Our job isn't to draw attention to ourselves so we can bask in praise and/or admired sympathy from onlookers. Our job is to obey Him! We're to obey Him at every point. We're to obey Him in every detail. We're to obey Him without a lot of arguing, whining, and complaining. Like John the Baptist, "I must decrease so He can increase!" Sometimes our "decreasing" goes on and on until we think there'll be nothing left! We can't let our ego dictate. God must be in control!

That's hard because Christ might decide to assign us some humble chore that we'd consider beneath our dignity. Satan is always there ready to plead our case for us about how mistreated and misunderstood we've been and how unfair the treatment we're experiencing really is. He is quick to remind us that God has been unjust in what He has allowed to come into our lives. Keeping a right attitude is also a big part of "spiritual warfare." If we indulge in self-pity and steep ourselves in remorse over what should've been and what might've been, we'll soon sink into a quagmire of bitterness that will eventually destroy us. Bitterness is an acid that will only destroy the container. We're the container if we allow our spirits to get bitter. A bitter spirit won't help God or anyone else, but it will certainly destroy us and neutralize our effectiveness for Jesus Christ.

I'll share a personal encounter with bitterness. I've pastored forty-four years, 37 of them in The Church of the Nazarene. I've been successful and have pastored some good-sized churches. I remember standing in the foyer of one church in particular, Grace Church of the Nazarene in Cheyenne, Wyoming, and congratulating myself because I'd finally gotten to a level in ministry where I had staff. I didn't have to clean the church building on Saturdays. I had a weekly radio program. I didn't have to run every program if it was to succeed, and I was looked up to on the district because I was pastoring the biggest church. I sincerely thanked God for guiding my career as He had. I had no idea how pompous I was being. Don't think badly of me. Most pastors are motivated by such ideas from time to time in their ministries.

After three years, I moved to Phoenix, Arizona! Lots of pastors would enjoy a place like that! I had beautiful facilities to work with and should be able to do something great for God. I've already alluded some of my experiences in Phoenix, so I won't elaborate here. I spent eleven years in Phoenix, doing what I could to reach people and build a great church. I literally poured my life and efforts out for God at that church. At the close of that ministry, circumstances were such that I didn't get a call to another "fine church in the denomination." I knew I could handle any assignment the church and God would give me. Here I was, a seasoned, talented, sincere pastor with years of valuable experience that any church would find beneficial to their ministry, and any church should want to grab me up as quickly as they could. Nobody grabbed! I was fifty, and most churches wanted younger, better-looking, more energetic pastors. "Look God! This is me! I need a good church! I've been faithful! I still have an awful lot to offer You! Where do you want me to go to serve you? Certainly, in another big city situation since I know so much about urban ministry!"

So went my prayers and thoughts.

Why didn't the phone ring? Why didn't God do something now!

Nobody took advantage of such a fine pastor being available! Finally, I was appointed to the pulpit at Stevenson, Washington. *Appointed!* And to a little country church! How could this be? I was a city pastor! I knew my way around in the big city! Now here I was at this little bitty country church! I was upset to think that this was the same kind of little church that I'd started ministry in thirty years before. This was not fair! I was embarrassed! I was certain everyone that I knew would think that I had bombed! After such a fine career, I'm a failure!

What's this? Am I detecting bitterness? Who could help it?

I must tell you that what I'm saying doesn't reflect upon the congregation at Stevenson Church of the Nazarene. They're wonderful people, and I love them! I couldn't ask for a finer congregation to work with in the building of God's kingdom.

And now I realize that I was also privileged to live in one of the most beautiful places in God's creation—the Columbia River Gorge! I was frustrated because I felt I was being "wasted" in a little church when I knew I had so much to offer and that I could pastor a bigger church!

One day, I was "praying?" Actually, I was on my knees complaining to God about how I'd been mistreated. I was having a real "pity party!" Suddenly, as I came up for breath, God spoke to me clearly. He said, *I thought that I called you to preach!*

I said, *You did, Lord.*

He said, *I thought you promised that you would go wherever I sent you!*

I answered, *I did Lord.*

He responded, *Then what is the problem?*

I answered, *Excuse me Lord, I guess there isn't one!*

My problem was I wanted to serve God in my way, a way that would bring comfort and glory to me. I had certain plans of my own! I'd earned the right to some security in my ministry. I didn't want to have to find extra work to support my wife, and I didn't want her to have to work to support me! I wanted people to recognize how really good I was at pastoring.

But God wanted to put me where He felt He could use me and where I'd be the most productive. He must've thought that since I belonged to Him that He had a right to use me as He saw fit. We weren't seeing eye to eye on this matter. Finally, when He got my attention, I was able to put away my foolish ego and submit in obedience to His Will. I must tell you I've been much happier about my assignment since I decided to obey God and not try to plan my own program! *Obedience is better than sacrifice and to hearken than the fat of rams!* Doing God's will does bring peace and fulfillment to life!

No matter how much potential we think we have, we'll be useless to God until we decide to obey His will one hundred percent! We preach entire sanctification, but we don't have the experience until we've said, "Yes, Lord, not my will, but thine!"

We find victory when we relinquish control to Him! That is when we become usable instruments for His glory!

When you look at the whole panorama and get things in perspective, you'll find that your place in "spiritual warfare" is to be exactly where God wants you to be, doing exactly what He wants you to do!

Jesus said, "I am the vine, ye are the branches: he that abideth in me, and I in him, the same bringeth forth much fruit: for without me ye can do nothing" (John 15:5)

We're in a war! We're living in very difficult days. There are even more difficult days coming! It's going to take every effort we can muster to maintain our Christian experience! But we can do it with Christ's power. *There is still power in the Blood!*

BIBLIOGRAPHY

Bible, King James Version, Cambridge University Press, Bentley House, 200 Euston Road, London, England

Beacon Bible Commentary, Beacon Hill Press, Kansas City, Missouri, 1965

Brown, Rebecca, M.D., *HE CAME TO SET THE CAPTIVES FREE*, Whitaker House, Springdale, PA., 1992

Brown, Rebecca, M.D., *PREPARE FOR WAR*, Chick Publications, Chino, California, 1987

Brown, Rebecca, M.D., *BECOMING A VESSEL OF HONOR*, Whitaker House, Springdale, PA., 1992

Purkiser, W.T., Ph.D., editor, *EXPLORING OUR CHRISTIAN FAITH*, Beacon Hill Press, Kansas City, Mo., 1960